For Maureen

PASSING TRAINS

THE CHANGING FACE OF CANADIAN RAILROADING

The BOSTON
MILLS PRESS

Canadian Cataloguing in Publication Data

McDonnell, Greg, 1954-
Passing trains: the changing face of Canadian railroading

ISBN 1-55046-183-4

1. Railroads-Canada-History.
2. Railroads-Canada-History-Pictorial works. I. Title.
TF26.M34 1996   385'.0971'09   C96-930708-X

Copyright© Greg McDonnell, 1996

David P. Morgan quotations from the April 1954 issue of
TRAINS magazine and *Canadian Steam!* (Kalmbach 1961) appear
with the permission of Kalmbach Publishing Co.

First published in 1996 by
The Boston Mills Press
132 Main Street
Erin, Ontario, Canada
N0B 1T0
Tel (519) 833-2407
Fax (519) 833-2195

An affiliate of
Stoddart Publishing Company Ltd.
34 Lesmill Road
North York, Ontario, Canada
M3B 2T6

Design
Sue Breen and Chris McCorkindale
McCorkindale Advertising & Design

Copy editing
Gordon Turner

Printed in China by
Book Art Inc., Toronto

The publisher gratefully acknowledges the support
of the Canada Council and Ontario Arts Council in the
development of writing and publishing in Canada.

JACKET:
At 2025, January 14, 1990, VIA No. 9, *The Canadian*, stops at Parry Sound for the last time.
Greg McDonnell

REAR JACKET:
Detroit-bound C&O symbol freight DT-41 blurs past the semaphores at BX Tower
in St. Thomas, Ontario, on a rainy autumn night in 1981. *Greg McDonnell*

PAGE 1
Frost coats a CPR switch lock at Galt, Ontario, on December 13, 1983. *Greg McDonnell*

PAGE 2
CP M636 4718 and M630 4563 idle impatiently as Toronto-bound No. 907 awaits the signal
to depart St. Luc, Quebec, at 1945, September 29, 1993. *Greg McDonnell*

PAGE 3
Having just hooped orders to CN Extra 1352 North on July 16, 1980, the Morris, Manitoba,
operator and his son return to the station. *Greg McDonnell*

PAGE 160
Silhouetted by the headlight of C&O GP7 5732, a brakeman stands guard at the wye switch
at Eastend in Chatham, Ontario, as the C&O yard job makes a delivery to the CPR at 2108,
October 26, 1981. *Greg McDonnell*

Essays

Winds of Change

A bitter north wind, the bone-chilling harbinger of an approaching winter, howls across the empty prairie east of Hak, Saskatchewan. Threatening black clouds spill over the horizon, contrasting sharply with the rich hues of recently harvested wheat fields that glow a radiant amber in the low autumn sun. Out of the west, a lonesome whistle calls and a thin red line advances slowly across the prairie. The low chant of a normally aspirated 645 engine and the comforting clickety-clack of steel wheels on jointed rail blend in soul-satisfying harmony as CP Rail GP38-2 3078 ambles eastward along the Shamrock Subdivision with a short string of 40-foot boxcars in tow. Hauling ten empty grain boxes billed to the elevators at McMahon, CP Work Extra 3078 is the quintessence of old-order prairie railroading. However, on October 16, 1995, the winds that blow across this subdivision herald not only the change of seasons, but permanent change.

In the wake of railway deregulation and the abolition of the famed Crows Nest Pass Agreement (which has regulated freight rates on grain and flour since 1897), the entire grain-transportation infrastructure is changing. Low-density branches on the prairie, particularly those restricted to boxcar loading, are doomed. Most will not survive the winter, and for the Shamrock, this is surely the last harvest.

So it is that we found ourselves following Work Extra 3078 over the Shamrock Subdivision, pushing our rented Chevy to the limit on the

At left: East of Hak, Saskatchewan, on the Shamrock Sub., CP Work Extra 3078 heads for McMahon with ten empty grain boxes at 1458, October 16, 1995. *Greg McDonnell*

Under threatening skies, loaded grain boxes line the elevator track at McMahon, Saskatchewan, on October 16, 1995. *Greg McDonnell*

back roads and gumbo dirt tracks of southern Saskatchewan. The road to McMahon is an unlikely place to encounter a pair of vagabonds from the east. However, Jim Brown and I were not there by chance, but in a race against time.

Steel wheels squeal in protest as the 3078 shoves 17 cars through the weed-grown elevator track at McMahon. It's a timeless ritual; just as previous generations of Geeps, Pacifics, Consolidations and Ten-Wheelers have done here for decades, the ten-year-old Dash 2 sets to the business of spotting empties at the Pioneer and Saskatchewan Pool elevators and lifting loads. CP Rail-painted boxcars and the 1985-vintage GP38-2 notwithstanding, watching the peddler work McMahon is like stepping back in time.

Westbound in the rain, Work Extra 3078 approaches Mileage 100.9 on the Shamrock Subdivision at 1548, October 16, 1995. *Greg McDonnell*

An icy rain begins to spatter as the conductor moves along the car tops, releasing handbrakes as he goes. On the ground, brakeman Rhonda Millar restores the derail, but the air of timelessness is broken as she hangs an SBU on the rear coupler of CP 18530, the last car of the cabooseless local. The intrusion of electronic technology is an instant reminder that what we have travelled several thousand miles to see, experience and document is the close of another chapter in Canadian railroading.

As the 3078 pulls out of McMahon with seven loads of No. 2 Red Wheat, the heavens unleash a torrential downpour. In the cold driving rain, the peddler heads for home. Rain streaks down the riveted sides of the aging cars as they rumble past us at Mileage 100.9, rocking and swaying their way

toward Hak. Watching the short train fade in the distance stirs the sudden realization that with the demise of the once-ubiquitous 40-foot boxcar, one of the last standards of old-order railroading will pass into history.

In this age of third-generation diesels, computer-aided CTC dispatching, double-stacks, RoadRailers and unit trains, SBU's, GBO's, DOB's and TOP's, the face and very fabric of Canadian railroading have changed. Although it was the single most dramatic change, dieselization was just the beginning. As the nation's steam locomotives dropped their fires for the last time, the new order sparked a technological revolution that continues to rage unabated. At the same time, air travel, trucking, automobiles and heavily subsidized highways took their toll. For dozens of passenger trains, hundreds

of miles of branch lines and thousands of railroad jobs across the nation, the combination proved fatal.

From Saint John and St. John's, to Prince Rupert, Penticton and Port Alberni, train-off notices were plastered on bulletin boards and station doors. The mixed train became all but extinct and even nationalization of the country's rail passenger network could not stem the decline. Under the VIA flag, train cancellations continued and even the legendary *Canadian* has been axed. Diverted to an all-CN routing, the train lives on in name only. The "Freight Only" signs have been hung out in Thunder Bay, Brandon, Broadview and Regina, Moose Jaw, Swift Current, Medicine Hat and Calgary; the stainless-steel streamliner no longer calls at Banff, nor snakes through Kicking Horse Canyon on its way to the Pacific.

Abandonments have decimated the nation's once extensive network of branch lines. Every mile of railroad on Prince Edward Island and the entire Newfoundland narrow gauge has been abandoned. The last trains have been OS'ed from Bridgewater, St. Quentin and Yarmouth, Upper Musquodoboit, Pugwash and Buctouche. In Quebec's Eastern Townships, nature is slowly reclaiming much of the Quebec Central, along with branch lines spiked down by the Grand Trunk and its predecessors in the previous century. Ontario's Bruce Peninsula, once a maze of CN and CP branch lines, is nearly devoid of trackage; the majority of branches in the rest of the province haven't fared much better. On the prairies, the "killing of the Crow" has sealed the fate of hundreds of miles of branch lines—and with them, uncounted elevators, small towns and line-side settlements.

Still, railroading remains a vibrant and vital artery of Canadian commerce…and an essential element of the Canadian experience. Full-cowl HR616's and zebra-striped SD's haul double-stack container trains westward from the Port of Halifax and LRC's whisk passengers from Toronto to Montreal in just 3 hours and 59 minutes. Battle-scarred SD40-2's thunder across the prairie with 14,000-ton trains of export grain, and brutish

AC4400-CW's lug trainloads of Kootenay coal to the Pacific tidewater. From the ashes of unwanted branch lines and downgraded mains, a new breed of service-driven, customer-oriented regional and short-line railroads are emerging. Goderich–Exeter; Central Western; Cape Breton & Central Nova Scotia; Windsor & Hantsport; New Brunswick Southern; Canadian American, et al., have revitalized once marginal operations with enthusiasm and independent spirit unseen on some lines since the original charters were granted.

In the fight to survive against ever tougher competition, railroads have jettisoned tradition, embracing new ways and new technology. The evolution of motive power and rolling stock has been closely watched and well documented, but what of the standard appurtenances, appliances, accoutrements and fixtures that we once took for granted? Wig-wags, semaphores, interlocking towers and stations; RPO's, ice-cooled reefers and steam-heated passenger cars; motor cars, auxiliaries and "splinter fleet" OCS equipment; grain doors, stock pens and stock cars; wooden mileposts and mile-boards—and crossbucks stencilled "RAILWAY CROSSING"; train orders and train-order hoops, whistle signals, white flags, kerosene marker lamps and even the Uniform Code of Operating Rules: all have either vanished or stand on the verge of extinction.

New technology and work rules have dehumanized railroading to a great extent. Local section crews have been widely dispersed and largely replaced by mechanized equipment and system gangs. Scores of roundhouses and shops have been closed, dozens of division points have been eliminated and dispatching offices have been centralized. Stations, once the centre of activity, have been closed and demolished by the hundreds; station agents and operators are virtually extinct. Faceless electronic devices known as SBU's or "Freds" have replaced the familiar caboose and the friendly nod from the rear of passing trains. However, in a ritual as old as railroading, children still wave as locomotives thunder past and engineers almost always wave back.

With a blinking SBU hung on the rear of CP 18530, Work Extra 3078 clatters past Mileage 100.9 on the Shamrock Sub. Loaded with No. 2 Red Wheat, the train's seven 40-foot grain boxes are destined for the Saskatchewan Pool elevators at Thunder Bay, Ontario. *Greg McDonnell*

Though the traditions and physical elements of the old order may fade away, the excitement, intrigue and captivating charm of railroading will not. Standing in the rain at Hak, we watch from a distance as Rhonda Millar lines the junction switch for the Swift Current–Meyronne Vanguard Subdivision, a branch with a somewhat brighter future. As if moving back through a time warp, Work Extra 3078 leaves the past behind as it exits the Shamrock Sub. Millar locks the switch behind the small train and the peddler departs for Swift Current. Knowing that within months the junction switch at Hak will be lined and locked for the Vanguard for good instills a sense of finality and underscores the urgency and import of our pilgrimage.

In essence, the objectives of this book parallel those of our mission to McMahon. Exploring these pages should be an adventure: a step back in time for an intimate look at old-order railroading and a journey forward, tracing the ties that bind past and present. On the road to McMahon, we were confined to the gumbo back roads and spindly rails of the Shamrock Sub. This volume is restricted by no such boundaries. Drawing upon the experiences of a thousand journeys, the efforts of some of the most talented railroad photographers in the world and no small amount of imagination, this book is a time machine set to embark on a trans-Canada journey through the distant and not-so-distant past, to see, experience and document railroading through an unforgettable season of change. All aboard!

A Mari Usque ad Mare

I am neither a prophet nor the son of a prophet, yet...I believe that many in this room will live to hear the whistle of a steam engine in the passes of the Rocky Mountains, and to make the journey from Halifax to the Pacific in five to six days.

Joseph Howe, Mason's Hall,
Halifax, May 15, 1851

Canada had yet to achieve nationhood and the CPR was not even dreamed of when Joseph Howe made his outrageous forecast of transcontinental travel. Less than 35 years later, Howe's foresight— if not a prophecy—was fulfilled as Donald Smith drove home a plain iron spike at Craigellachie, British Columbia, at 9:22 a.m., November 7, 1885.

The ceremony marked completion of the Canadian Pacific Railway, an iron road uniting the young nation "from Sea to Sea."

In the jet age, the outrageousness of Howe's prediction is lost on most Canadians, who expect to get from Halifax to the Pacific in a little more than six hours, not five or six days. However, on a frigid night in March 1975, an airline strike has grounded the nation's fleets of DC9's and B-727's, stranding travellers in airports, hotels and the homes of in-laws. Suddenly, the phones in railway ticket agencies are ringing off the hook.

In the sub-zero darkness of an unseasonably cold night, CP E8 1800 and RS10 8574 pause at McAdam, New Brunswick, with Saint John–Montreal train 41, *The Atlantic Limited*. All available space in sleepers *Chateau Bienville* and *Fraser Manor* has been sold and it's standing room only in Skyline car 515 and coach 125. By morning, the train will be in Montreal. Connecting with *The Canadian* at Montreal's Windsor Station, those with through tickets to Vancouver will make the journey to the Pacific in just over three and a half days...by no means a remarkable achievement, but far better than those whose air-line tickets are good only for a night on the benches of the Saint John airport, or in some over-priced hotel. Somewhere, Joseph Howe is smiling.

Cab lights casting his shadow on the cars of a departing eastbound, the engineer of CP No. 41, *The Atlantic Limited*, reads over his train orders at McAdam, New Brunswick, on March 9, 1975. Slaking the thirst of the steam generators aboard E8 1800 and RS10 8574, McAdam roundhouse workers top off the units' water tanks before No. 41 resumes its journey on an unseasonably cold night. *Greg McDonnell*

Lifting out of Halifax, Nova Scotia, CN HR616 2104, secondhand SD40-2 6093 (still in UP paint), HR616 2116, M636 2325 and M420 3573 duck under the Marlborough Woods overpass with Toronto-bound container train No. 207 at 1950, June 5, 1994. *Greg McDonnell*

Idling on the ready tracks at CN's Fairview roundhouse in Halifax, Nova Scotia, C630M's 2038 and 2009 await the call to duty on September 29, 1980. *Greg McDonnell*

Fulfilling their intended role, CN RSC13's 1711, 1713 and 1704 tiptoe across the wooden trestle at Tracadie, New Brunswick, with the Caraquet Sub. local in May 1975. Nearing the end of their career, the venerable 1700's will soon be retired and surrender their A1A trucks to an RS18 rebuild program that will produce a new class of lightweight road-switchers to take their place on Maritime branches with light axle-loading restrictions. *Stan J. Smaill*

Just out of French Village, Nova Scotia, CN RSC13 1728 leads Yarmouth–Halifax mixed train M244 past Mileage 15 on the Chester Subdivision on October 8, 1966. Express reefers on the head end are undoubtedly loaded with fish, long a staple of traffic on the former Halifax & Southwestern. *James A. Brown*

Lost in the Land of Evangeline

Dominion Atlantic Railway. The very name is enchanting. In the flesh, CP's 300-mile Nova Scotia subsidiary—linked to Canadian Pacific proper by CPSS Bay of Fundy steamships—was irresistible.

Even minus the high-stepping G2-class Pacifics, venerable D10's and polished tuscan-red passenger trains that endeared the DAR to generations, the Land of Evangeline Route remained one of CP's most engaging properties. Budd RDC's slipped past Annapolis Valley orchards, sliced through picturesque villages and soared over tidal waters on bridges of concrete and steel. Assigned to the road's Kentville shops, DAR's "own" (albeit lettered CP)

SW1200's patrolled the main from Yarmouth to Windsor Jct., worked the mixed to Truro and the branches to Centreville, Kingsport and Weston.

Though the Land of Evangeline crest was last seen on the tenders of D10's and G2's, the DAR maintained a good measure of independence. The railway was headquartered, managed and dispatched from offices in the rambling, two-storey frame station at Kentville. The equipment may have been lettered Canadian Pacific, but to railroaders and residents alike, the CPR was somewhere on the other side of the Bay of Fundy; *their* railway was—and always would be—the Dominion Atlantic.

Spring is in the air as a lone CP Dayliner skirts

the shore of the Annapolis Basin near Deep Rock, Nova Scotia. For the few passengers aboard CP RDC1 9062 on April 25, 1975, DAR train No. 2 offers little more than basic transportation. However, the countryside rolling past the Budd car's picture windows is ample compensation for the lack of amenities.

The view from DAR No. 2 may be pleasant, but in Windsor Station, CPR accountants see only ink as red as the letter boards of the 9062. In the spring of 1975, No. 2 and the DAR itself are in danger. Indeed, the Halifax–Yarmouth RDC's and the DAR will cling to life for just 15 more years. Freight service west of Middleton ended on December 20, 1989, and on January 14, 1990, the 9062's sister car, VIA 6142 (ex-CP 9061), accompanied RDC1 6119 on VIA No. 154, the last Yarmouth–Halifax passenger train.

Sustained by Mantua–Hantsport gypsum traffic, the New Minas–Windsor Jct. "east end" of the DAR survives as the Windsor & Hantsport. West of Mileage 55, just outside Kentville, the rails are gone. Whistles no longer echo through the orchards of the Annapolis and no more do trains call on Aylesford, Church Point, or Meteghan, Yarmouth, Kentville or Annapolis Royal. The last passengers have made their across-the-pier connection with *Princess Helene* and *Princess of Acadia* at Digby. A weed-grown roadbed, rotting ties and crumbling concrete bridge abutments remain, but railroading is lost forever in the Land of Evangeline.

Skirting the shore of the Annapolis Basin near Deep Brook, Nova Scotia, Dominion Atlantic No. 2, with CP RDC1 9062, heads for Halifax on April 25, 1975. *Greg McDonnell*

In the last light of day, Windsor & Hantsport RS23's 8027, 8046 and 8026, all still in CP Rail paint, roll gypsum gons over a tributary of the Avon River near Windsor, Nova Scotia, on August 29, 1994. *Tom Lambrecht*

Coupled behind wooden van 437130, CP heavyweight coach 1303 carries the markers as Truro–Windsor mixed M22 drifts through Clarksville, Nova Scotia, on April 24, 1975. Remarkably, the Truro mixed survived into the VIA era and was not discontinued until the end of April 1979. CP 1303, one of fifteen 1929-vintage heavyweight coaches built at National Steel Car and completed at Angus Shops, is still in existence. Christened the *Micmac*, the car is stored in Ottawa, Ontario, as part of the National Museum of Science and Technology excursion train. *Greg McDonnell*

Last Train to Clarksville

There was a time when mixed trains were a staple of rural railroading. Across the nation, from Carbonear to Cranbrook, Camrose and Cranberry Portage, combines and heavyweight coaches were coupled to the rear of local freights and timecarded as "mixed train service." By definition, the mixed was a notoriously poor timekeeper, but an invariably friendly conveyance. Dominion Atlantic M21/M22, the Truro–Windsor, Nova Scotia, mixed was such a train. In 1975, it was also the last mixed train service carded by the "World's Greatest Travel System."

CP Rail was not about to advertise or acknowledge the train's existence. The Truro–Windsor mixed was absent from the company's system timetable. DAR public timetables listed the service, but provided no schedule or list of stations, just a short notice reading: "Windsor and Truro Trains M21 and M22. Mixed train service (carrying passengers). Full particulars may be obtained from your local Dominion Atlantic Railway Agent."

In Windsor, "your local Dominion Atlantic Railway Agent" was the station operator, who informed us that M21 would depart sometime around 1700. Pounding the validator, he issued a pair of one-way tickets to Clarksville, and Andrew Sutherland and I were granted passage back in time.

Sandwiched between an empty CP boxcar and an aging wooden van, heavyweight coach 1303 provided accommodation on M21. An 83-foot 10-inch, 12-wheeled battleship of a car, CP 1303 had changed little in nearly a half-century of service.

From her rich mahogany panelling, to rows of green plush walkover seats, the venerable coach was a survivor, an enduring symbol of the rock-solid stability of the company whose name was spelled out across her letter boards: CANADIAN PACIFIC.

Twenty-six cars separated the 1303 from the head end, but there was minimal slack action as the engineer notched out on the throttle of SW1200RS 8136 and coaxed the train into motion. The old car creaked and groaned in protest as the mixed moved through the yard, but once on the main, the 1303 rode and sounded as if she could roll on forever.

With just three revenue passengers aboard, the 1303 looked empty, but the ancient heavyweight was crowded with memories. Memories of uncounted millions of miles rolled off in the consists of everything from prestigious name trains to lowly locals; of untold thousands of passengers—young and old; rich and poor; family, friends and lovers—who have settled back in her plush cushions, travelling to wed, to work and to war; on honeymoons, holidays and home again. Like a tuscan-painted time machine, CP 1303 rolled back the years as she clicked off the miles.

Clarksville, Mileage 18.7 on the Truro Subdivision, came all too soon and M21 screeched to a perfect passenger-train stop directly in front of the big white house that fronted on the tracks. We stepped off the train and back into the real world. With the sigh of releasing brakes and a wave from the van, M21 rolled into oblivion.

Almost all of CP 1303's 82 green plush walkover seats are empty, but, after nearly a half century of service, the elderly coach is crowded with memories. A tuscan-painted, mahogany-panelled time machine, the heavyweight coach is assigned to Truro–Windsor, Nova Scotia, mixed-train service on April 24, 1975. *Greg McDonnell*

The youngest of the legendary trio of CPR 4-4-0's assigned to Chipman, New Brunswick, A1e No. 29 (CP Delormier Shops 1887) pauses at the water tank at Perry, New Brunswick, with Chipman–Norton mixed train No. 560 on October 8, 1959. In deference to light axle loadings and frail bridges on the Chipman-Norton portion of Minto Subdivision, CPR 4-4-0's 29, 136 and 144 survived long after the American Standard type vanished from the roster of virtually every other Class 1 road in North America. The tiny 4-4-0's were finally replaced by CLC diesel hydraulic No. 18 in the fall of 1959. While the Minto Subdivision and No. 18 are long gone, all three of the famed Eight-Wheelers have been preserved. No. 136 is in excursion service on the South Simcoe Railway at Tottenham, Ontario; No. 144 is on display at the Canadian Railway Museum in Delson, Quebec, and No. 29, operational until damaged by a 1994 fire at the Salem & Hillsborough Railroad in Hillsborough, New Brunswick, is awaiting restoration. *Robert R. Malinoski*

Making its traditional across-the-platform connection, CN No. 333 meets No. 59, *The Scotian,* at Oxford Jct., Nova Scotia, on May 20, 1960. With H12-64 1624, a wooden RPO and a steel combine substituting for the carded "motor car train," the local will make the 69.2-mile return trip to Pictou as No. 334. One of only thirty CLC H12-64's (all delivered to CN), 1624 was retired in 1968 as CN purged all F-M power from its roster. The lead unit on No. 59, FPA4 6766 was destroyed in a head-on collision on the Drummondville (Quebec) Subdivision in November 1967. *James A. Brown*

Operating as No. 908, the McAdam plow is in the clear at 1610, March 9, 1975, as No. 907 hurtles through Harvey, New Brunswick, shoving the disabled Plow Extra 8448 West. After limping into Fredericton Jct. on just one traction motor, the 8448 was coaxed westward until rescued by RS18's 8744 and 8787 on Montreal-bound road freight 907. *Greg McDonnell*

A casualty of the rigours of snowplow service, CP RS3 8448 thaws in the roundhouse at McAdam, New Brunswick, on March 9, 1975. The freshly overhauled RS3 lost all but one traction motor to ground relays while working a plow extra east of Saint John, and was assisted into McAdam by No. 907. *Greg McDonnell*

Of Poets and Prime Ministers

In the still of a moonless June night, a trio of big Alcos prowl through the darkness of D Yard in Truro, Nova Scotia. The gruff talk of V16 251's echoes across the nearly vacant yard. A dimmed headlight, illuminated number boards and the bobbing white light of a brakeman's lantern etch the blackness as the burly Centuries grope in the dark for their train. The metallic crash of mating couplers sounds across the yard, and from somewhere, a radio crackles. "Good joint, 408, take 'em ahead." Lumbering forward, the big C's ease into the yellow glow of the yard-office lights and stop.

Their freshly scrubbed flanks glistening in the warm cast of sodium lights, the veteran MLW's bear traces of their CN heritage, but they proudly

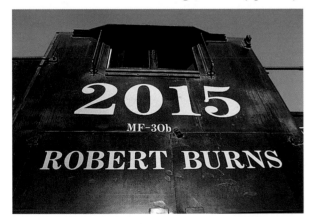

wear a large red lion rampant and the name of their new owner emblazoned across their hoods: Cape Breton & Central Nova Scotia Railway. Taken from the coats of arms of Nova Scotia and Scotland, the lion rampant pays tribute to the region's Scottish heritage, but it is equally symbolic of the spirit and fierce independence of the CB&CNS and its people.

Part of the shortline empire of Texas-based RailTex, the Cape Breton & Central Nova Scotia took over CN's 236-mile Truro–Sydney operation on October 1, 1993. With the new ownership came new management, a new way of doing business, and Mark Westerfield, a Wisconsin native as well versed in literature and history as railroading. As the first CB&CNS General Manager, Westerfield helped instill a sense of pride and an independent spirit that has revolutionized and revitalized Cape Breton railroading.

Honouring an age-old tradition, revived by Westerfield, all CB&CNS locomotives carry names, as well as road numbers. The Cape Breton road's eight ex-CN C630M's are named after Scottish poets and novelists, while the five CB&CNS RS18's carry the names of Canadian prime ministers—three of them from Nova Scotia. The aging MLW's are at home on the Cape Breton

line, which has been Alco country since CN FA's, RS3's and RS10's bumped ex-CGR Mikes and ancient 2-8-0's from the Highlands more than three decades ago. On the legendary grades at River Denys and Marshy Hope, the performance of these elderly freighters is as spectacular as the battles once waged there by double-shotted government road Mikados and braces of green-and-gold RS3's.

Outside the Truro yard office, the engineer of Sydney-bound No. 408 releases the brakes and slowly notches out the throttle of C630M 2032 *Lord Byron*. Shouting into the night, *Lord Byron*, *Robert Burns* and *William Dunbar* dig in. The staccato bark of V-16 Alco 251's rattles the yard office windows and shatters the Saturday night stillness of the small Nova Scotia town. With all of the authority and urgency of the fast freights of old, the big C's hustle 408 into the darkness, racing toward the dawn of a new day...and the dawn of a new age of Maritime railroading.

At right: Proudly bearing the lion rampant on its flanks, CB&CNS C630M 2032 *Lord Byron* (ex-CN 2032) awaits the highball to head east with Sydney-bound road freight No. 408 at 2300, June 4, 1994. *Greg McDonnell*

Returning to Stellarton after delivering coal to the power plant at Trenton, the CB&CNS "afternoon shunter," with freshly painted RS18 3627 *Sir John A. Macdonald* and CN 1765, passes the courthouse at New Glasgow, Nova Scotia, at 1950, June 4, 1994. *Greg McDonnell*

Leaning from the cab of aging Devco RS1 207, a veteran hostler shuffles the 1944-vintage Alco along the shop track at Glace Bay, Nova Scotia, on May 13, 1975. *Philip Mason*

Facing an ancient slide-valve switcher, Sydney & Louisburg 2-8-2 No. 76 simmers on the shop track at Glace Bay, Nova Scotia, on May 19, 1960. Notable for its stable of oddball wheel arrangements and hand-me-down power from at least half a dozen U.S. roads, the Cape Breton coal hauler was one of the last steam strongholds in North America. *James A. Brown*

The lower quadrant train-order signal—a legacy of the Reid Newfoundland era—displays clear as CN NF110 907 and NF210's 919, 943 and 927 pass the old wooden depot at Gambo, Newfoundland, with trans-island freight No. 204 on May 10, 1975. *Philip Mason*

Nevermore Newfoundland

I 'll say this is the end of the line." Choking back emotion, Monroe Greening, the engineer on CN Extra 944 East got up from his seat at the throttle and closed another chapter of Newfoundland railroading. Booking off at Clarenville, he passed the final Bishop's Falls–St. John's freight to its last crew. Standing in the rain, NF210's 944, 941, 936, 945 and 946, two gons of scrap, three empty flats, an OCS tank car and caboose 6054, waited to resume their sombre journey to St. John's. Trans-island service on the 547-mile narrow-gauge railway began on June 29, 1898; it would end with the small train's arrival in the Newfoundland capital on September 29, 1988.

One day later, the island province played host to its final regular trains, the Bishop's Falls–Corner Brook mixed trains. The last vestige of trans-island fast freights 203 and 204, the trains had precious little tonnage to move since container traffic was diverted to trucks in July. On September 30, 1988, No. 203, Passenger Extra 917 West, left Bishop's Falls for the last time with five units and a pair of cabooses bracketing two coaches and a baggage car.

While the mood in the cab of NF210 917 was subdued, the train's crowded coaches swayed to the rhythm of accordion music. Passengers sang, and drinks and stories of better days flowed freely as Newfoundlanders bid goodbye to their railroad. In the words of passenger Steve Bradley, "It was more like an Irish wake than a last run." There would be plenty of time to mourn later.

At the stroke of midnight, October 1, 1988, the former Newfoundland Railway was formally abandoned. Still miles from its destination at the appointed hour, Passenger Extra 939 East, with

Conductor A. C. Dillon, Engineer Ray Boyd and 102 passengers, rolled toward Bishop's Falls on a railroad that had officially ceased to exist. Arriving at Bishop's Falls in the wee hours, the former No. 204 closed out 107 years of railroad service in Newfoundland. The next morning, work trains set to the grim task of assisting with the dismantling of the railroad.

It's been said that by cashing in the money-losing railway for $800 million in highway funds,

politicians sold the soul of the island province in a backroom deal cut to achieve short-term gains for a few individuals—at the expense of irreparable longterm losses for Newfoundland. The full story may never be known, but history will record that in a bittersweet ceremony held at 1410 NST, Wednesday, October 12, 1988, workers removed the first spike from the Newfoundland Railway at Mileage 339.8, between Gaff Topsail and Kitty's Brook. Railroading on the Rock was history.

With Monroe Greening at the throttle, CN (Terra Transport) Extra 944 East, the last trans-island train, trudges through the rain-soaked forest west of Clarenville, Newfoundland, on September 29, 1988. *Steve Bradley*

Barely polished by the passage of mixed train No. 205, the rails of the Bonavista Subdivision bask in the summer sun as CN G8's 803 and 801 negotiate the Trinity Loop en route to Bonavista, Newfoundland, on July 30, 1980. The Bonavista branch was abandoned on June 20, 1984, but the Trinity Loop has been preserved as the Clayton D. Cook Loop Railroad. Equipment on display at the historic site includes G8 802, two cabooses and a number of passenger and freight cars. CN 803 is on display at Carbonear, Newfoundland, while sister 805 forms part of a narrow-gauge display at the Canadian Railway Museum in Delson, Quebec. *Joe McMillan*

Tracing the rocky shoreline at Seal Cove, Newfoundland, CN G8's 800 and 802 and three cars head for the Argentia Sub. with mixed train No. 207 on July 27, 1984. The Argentia–Carbonear mixed made its last run on September 20, 1984. *Joe McMillan*

From Izma's to the Island

TRAINS. The bright red-and-white logo of the magazine displayed high on the shelf in Izma's Five Points (my Uncle Joe's grocery store and soda bar) immediately caught my eye. Standing on tiptoes, I excitedly pulled the September 1963 issue of TRAINS magazine from the shelf, revealing a Jim Shaughnessy cover shot of three CNR GE 70-tonners in the shop at Charlottetown, Prince Edward Island. To an eight-year-old, the price was high, but for 50 cents, I purchased my first copy of TRAINS and established a lifetime relationship with "*the* magazine of railroading." In retrospect, it was the best 50 cents I've ever spent.

In the monthly pages of TRAINS (as well as treasured back issues), I found more than news, knowledge and photographs. The influential works of David P. Morgan, Philip Hastings, Jim Shaughnessy, Richard Steinheimer, J. Parker Lamb and many others gave me the motivation to pursue my own photographic and journalistic goals. From the legendary Morgan and Hastings "In Search of Steam," "Smoke over the Prairies," and "Steam in Indian Summer" series, to the sensitive prose and exquisite photographs of Ted Benson, TRAINS was a constant and guiding source of inspiration. Understandably, I had a certain attachment to that Shaughnessy photograph, the P.E.I. cover shot that started it all.

It took a dozen years, but on April 28, 1975, I stepped into the same Charlottetown shop where Shaughnessy had exposed the memorable photograph. The green and gold paint was gone, but a

quartet of CN 70-tonners—including No. 35, one of the engines on the September 1963 cover—had been bedded down for the night. The last four 70-tonners on the CN roster, GE's 35, 30, 40 and

41 shared the Charlottetown shop with RSC13 1728 in a scene that instantly rekindled the excitement of that hot August evening at Izma's Five Points. Shaughnessy should have been there.

A shopman tends to his duties as CN GE 70-tonners 27, 28 and 35 congregate in the Charlottetown, Prince Edward Island, shop on August 15, 1962. All three units illustrated in this memorable image have been retired and scrapped. *Jim Shaughnessy*

Recreating the classic Shaughnessy scene, CN 35, 40, 30 and 41 (the last four 70-tonners on the roster), join RSC13 1728 in the Charlottetown, Prince Edward Island, shop on a spring evening. Preserved at the Canadian Railway Museum in Delson, Quebec, No. 30 is the sole survivor of the five units seen slumbering on April 28, 1975. *Greg McDonnell*

Passing freshly tilled fields, Borden-bound boat train No. 115 approaches Hunter River, Prince Edward Island, with CN RSC13's 1732 and 1733 leading a steam-generator car, two baggage cars, an RPO car and a single coach on May 3, 1968. Although passenger service on PEI would soon come to an end, island freights continued to make the car-ferry connection at Borden until A1A-trucked RS18's 1787 and 1750 loaded the last cars aboard the m.v. *Abegweit* on December 28, 1989, closing 114 years of railroading on Prince Edward Island. *William R. Linley*

Returning to Charlottetown with three 40-foot boxcars and a wooden van, CN GE 70-tonners 41 and 40 cross the Pisquid River on the Montague Sub. near Mt. Stewart Jct., Prince Edward Island, in September 1971. Due to frail bridges and light rail, the east end of the island province remained the exclusive domain of the little GE's until their retirement in the early 1980s. *William R. Linley*

Ice and heavy snow grip the wooden trestle over the Pisquid River as CN 70-tonners 41 and 35— braced for battle with drifts on the Montague and Murray Harbour Subdivisions—head east with a plow extra on February 7, 1974. *William R. Linley*

Riviere du Loup Revisited

Long past the witching hour on a stormy June night, the rain-slicked streets of Riviere du Loup, Quebec, are deserted. The air is still and but for the gentle patter of falling rain, the town is quiet. Slumbering by the old brick enginehouse at the CNR yard, a pair of RS18's await the call to duty, while the darkened shop beckons the curious visitor.

The doors of the old building are locked, but the ghosts that inhabit its dark recesses have been stirred; they capture the imagination and spirit the visitor back in time. In the rainy darkness, text memorized since childhood and photographs indelibly etched in a young mind come alive, conjuring visions of a cold November night when David P. Morgan and Philip Hastings, "a pair of nomads from dieseldom," called on Riviere du Loup in 1953.

For the visitor strolling slowly up the platform, Morgan's prose and Hastings's photos inspire vivid images of CNR U-2-e Northern 6179 paused at Riviere du Loup with the *Maritime Express* "surrounded by men furiously intent on what looked like 15-minute classified repairs; fire cleaners raking the grates, dislodging a torrent of ashes and fiery coals; the staccato pumping of the Alemite guns; blue flags on the pilot, a man on the Vanderbilt tank slaking an inevitable thirst." In the almost eerie silence, it's easy to imagine the big 4-8-4 simmering away, with air pumps thumping impatiently and steam hissing amid the "constant, animated yelling—conversing and jabbering in French" of hostlers and crewmen.

From out of the east, an air horn breaks the spell and the ghosts retreat to the shadows. The platform is empty and the rain continues to fall. A second horn calls out from the west and a stereophonic symphony of hammering Alco exhaust and wailing air horns erupts as the eastbound *Ocean* and its westbound counterpart approach Riviere du Loup simultaneously.

At exactly 0300, VIA Nos. 14 and 15, both led by MLW FPA4's, ease into Riviere du Loup and grind to a halt; No. 14 on the main, No. 15 in the siding. Seemingly out of nowhere, shop men descend upon the eastbound *Ocean*, watering the steam generator tanks of FPA4 6786 and FPB4 6861, checking over the units and inspecting cars. Steam swirls into the night sky, and Alco-design cabs, turned out by the same Montreal works that produced CNR 6179, idle impatiently while French-speaking hostlers and crewmen play out a scene strikingly similar to the ritual immortalized by Morgan and Hastings so long ago.

Two shrill blasts on the communication whistle sound in the cab of the 6786 signal a highball from the tail end of No. 14. The Alco 12-251B's throbbing inside the carbody units come to life and the *Ocean*'s blue-and-yellow consist, punctated by 6-6-4 sleeper *Green Bush*, slides gracefully into the night. As No. 14's markers dissolve into the darkness, brakemens' lanterns wave hand signals and radios crackle as No. 15 backs out of the siding and pulls up the main to make its station stop.

Seven cars from the head end of No. 15, VIA Daynighter 5724 offers refuge from the rain and a reclining seat. With a gentle tug, the Montreal-bound *Ocean* gets under way at 0345. The interior lights of the 5724 are turned low and the elderly car, rebuilt from 1954-vintage CN coach 5493, rides like a dream. Settled into a luxurious reclining seat, lulled by the rhythm of the rails and comforted by the renewed conviction that the magic of railroading transcends not only the passage of generations, but technological change, sleep comes easy.

Under the watchful eye of the head-end crew, machinists service CNR U-2-e Northern 6179 while No. 2, the eastbound *Maritime Express* makes its stop at Riviere du Loup, Quebec, at 8:10 p.m., November 1, 1953. *Philip R. Hastings*

At right: Conjuring visions of the *Maritime Express*, VIA No. 14, the *Ocean*, with FPA4 6786 and FPB4 6861, makes its stop at Riviere du Loup, Quebec, while No. 15, with FPA4 6789, F9B 6634 and FPB4 6871, waits on the siding at 0325, June 10, 1981. *Greg McDonnell*

On the longest day of the year, the setting sun probes the depths of the tunnel near Port Daniel, Quebec, as VIA FPA4 6770 bursts from the solid-rock bore with No. 17, the westbound *Chaleur* on June 21, 1988.
Robert Lambrecht

The deep blue waters of Chaleur Bay shimmer in the background as VIA F40PH-2 6428 leads No.16, the *Chaleur*, over a wooden trestle at L'Anse aux Gascons, Quebec, on September 18, 1989. *Hal Reiser*

Straining to hold back a 17,000-ton, 150-car train of iron ore, QCM M636's 81 and 74 thunder though the rock cuts north of Able, Quebec, at 1235, June 8, 1981. Helping to keep the heavy train stretched out, remote-control helper engine M636 47 is coupled on the rear of the train. *Greg McDonnell*

One for the Books

My old Grade 13 geography text described the Canadian Shield as a million square miles with a million lakes and a million rocky hills—a forbidding land of dense trackless forest and bald, hard-rock hills, the remains of Precambrian mountains ground to cores of granite and gneiss by ancient glaciers. From atop one of those million rocky hills, a worn granite outcropping in the Shield country north of Port Cartier, Quebec, the rugged beauty of the land is breathtaking. A gentle breeze wafts through scented forests of cedar, birch and pine, while the weathered hills, with jagged faces of sheer granite, reach for the sky. Far below, the seething black waters of the Riviere aux Rochers surge their way toward the St. Lawrence.

Carved into the ancient rock, steel rails cling to the hillside high above the river, as the Cartier Railway follows its own twisting course to the St. Lawrence. But for the occasional thump of heavy rails expanding in the midday heat, the Cartier is quiet. The serenity of this place, miles from the nearest road, fortifies the soul, but after an hour of peaceful reflection, the melodic call of a five-chime horn snaps me to attention.

Alco exhaust echoes down the canyon and within minutes, the bright orange face of Cartier M636 81 bursts from behind a rock wall. Straining to hold back a 19,000-ton downbound train, QCM 81 and sister 74 squeal into the tight curve in full dynamics. The whine of a dozen GE traction motors and the gruff talk of V16 251's reverberate through the rock cuts. In the wake of the brawny M-lines, 150 stubby ore cars snake through the sweeping S-curves, their precious cargo of sparkling ore concentrate bound for the hungry blast furnaces of steel mills in the industrial heartland.

Tapping the rich iron deposits of the Labrador–Quebec Trough, the 281-mile, Port Cartier–Mount Wright railway is an all-Alco, iron-ore conveyor belt moving train-loads of beneficiated ore from the mines to 150,000-tonne deadweight bulk carriers docked in Port Cartier harbour. One of the last bastions of six-motor Alco power on the continent, the Cartier is a spectacular stage for heavy-duty railroading, and that's something the old geography books neglected to mention.

With its cargo of beneficiated iron ore sparkling in the sun, a QCM southbound squeals through the curves near Mileage 11 on June 8, 1981. Still attired in factory-applied green and yellow, M636 74 was part of the second QCM order delivered from MLW in 1973, while the lead unit, QCM 81 was delivered as part of the final M636 order in 1975. *Greg McDonnell*

The gentle beat of a MacIntosh & Seymour 539 and the melodious call of a three-chime horn drift through the morning air as Alma & Jonquieres S4 102 ambles through La Chaine, Quebec, with Saguenay Power–Alma mixed train No. 2 on August 30, 1962. *Robert Sandusky*

A long way from Jamaica (New York, that is), Roberval & Saguenay C420 34—originally Long Island 214—leads M420TR 27 and RS18 24
on a Jonquiere-bound drag near La Baie, Quebec, in August, 1990. *Thomas L. Carver*

Sleepless in Megantic

Flickering red, yellow and green, kerosene switch lamps maintain their faithful vigil while fog swirls across the CPR yard in Megantic, Quebec, in the predawn hours of December 31, 1965. Ablaze in the brilliant glare of yard lights, the sky glows a surreal yellow, silhouetting the dark forms of freight cars, cabooses, slumbering snowplows and a lone steel combine.

Its passenger compartment warmed by an Eastman heater, heavyweight combine 3253 has spent the night in front of the station, having arrived from Brownville Jct., Maine, the previous evening on No. 517, "the Scoot." Within an hour, the car will be coupled to the rear of train 518, and RS3 8435 will hurry "the Scoot" back to Brownville Jct.

A fixture on CP's International of Maine, "the Scoot" has called on remote settlements, camps and cottages since the late 1800s, but on the last day of 1965, the legendary mixed is on borrowed time. Kept alive by a mail contract to serve isolated on-line communities, the Brownville Jct.–Megantic mixed will last but another year.

Although the future of the famed "Scoot" is as gloomy as the weather, the circumstances fail to dampen the spirits of young George Melvin, riding the mixed with his father on a Brownville Jct.–Megantic round trip planned for a year. The photographer vividly recounts the "wild east" atmosphere of Megantic, where the band playing directly below their trackside hotel room rocked well into the night and CPR trains rattled the windows long after last call. No matter, when *The Atlantic Limited*, with a tuscan-and-grey FPA2, an RS10 and an all-tuscan consist, is paused outside the window, sleep is out of the question.

At right: Lunch box and grip in hand, an outbound crewman waits on the platform at Megantic, Quebec, as Canadian Atlantic No. 281 rolls into town behind CP C424 4235, M630 4568 and another C424 on January 19, 1991. CP created the Canadian Atlantic Railway in 1988 as a prelude to spinning off its lines east of Sherbrooke. On January 6, 1995, the Canadian American Railroad assumed operation of line between Megantic and Brownville Jct., Maine, while Irving's New Brunswick Railway Company took over the remaining trackage from Brownville Jct. to Saint John. Operations on the Brownville Jct.–McAdam Mattawamkeag Sub. are contracted to the Canadian American, while all trackage east of McAdam is operated as the New Brunswick Southern. *Hal Reiser*

Maintaining their faithful vigil in the CP yard in Megantic, Quebec, kerosene switch lamps flicker in the predawn darkness on December 31, 1965. *George F. Melvin*

Stopped for a crew change on a July 1977 afternoon, CN C630M 2001 and three RS18's cool their wheels in front of the rambling two-storey depot at Monk, Quebec, a division point on the former National Transcontinental Railway. Through freights will soon be a rarity on this portion of the old NTR, as completion of the new Pelltier cutoff will siphon all but local traffic from the Monk Subdivision. *William R. Linley*

Rumbling across the Richelieu River bridge, CN C630M 2005, M636 2323 and C630M 2023 approach Beloeil, Quebec, with a Halifax–Montreal hotshot at 1400, February 21, 1978. CN's Richelieu crossing was made infamous at 1:15 a.m., June 29, 1864, when a Grand Trunk train carrying German immigrants to Montreal ran through an open draw and crashed onto a barge in the canal below. Ninety-nine people died in the accident that remains the worst in Canadian railway history. *Greg McDonnell*

The second-trick operator at Delson, Quebec, hoops orders to No. 35, the *Adirondack*, as D&H PA1u 16 eases the six-car train through the crossovers connecting D&H subsidiary Napierville Junction to CP's Adirondack Subdivision at 1927, August 23, 1975. *Greg McDonnell*

The station gardens are in full bloom as D&H RS2's 4021 and 4022 pause at Montreal West, Quebec, with NYC/D&H New York–Montreal overnighter, the *Montreal Limited*, in August 1962. *Robert Sandusky*

Montreal West Winters

Standing in the open vestibule of a heavyweight CPR coach, I held a tight grip on the handrail as the brakes grabbed hold and the westbound commuter train began to slow for a station stop. Snow sifted up between the cars and into the step wells; a crossing, then the lights of a station blurred past, and as the old car shuddered to a halt, I stepped onto the platform at Montreal West, Quebec, for the very first time.

Clouds of steam billowed about the big tuscan cars and snow squeaked underfoot as Stan Smaill and I hurried to the head end of the train, where CP E8A 1801 stared at the triple-aspect stop indication displayed by signal 47. The red signals cut laser-like beams through ice crystals suspended in the frigid air, while the ice-encrusted E, its twin 12-567B engines throbbing impatiently, held fast in compliance with Rule 292.

Up in Montreal West Tower, the operator pulled back on a pistol-grip lever and Signal 47 flashed to high-green. Crossing bells sounded their urgent warning and the gates guarding Westminster Avenue slowly descended. The 1801's headlight switched to bright, and, a notch at a time, the hogger wound out the 567-series V-12's powering his elegant charge. Making light work of her substantial consist of heavyweight coaches, the elderly E-unit made a dramatic exit and an indelible impression.

CPR's Montreal West station was just blocks from the Smaill home, and visits with Stan were synonymous with time spent at the classic four-track suburban depot. Rush-hour parades, with tuscan commuter trains led by beaver-crested FP7's; D&H PA's on the *Laurentian* and *Montreal Limited* and CP E8's on the Quebec City and Ottawa trains were regular highlights, but Montreal West was at its dramatic best in winter.

Montreal West winters meant walking to the station after supper to watch snow-packed D&H RS2's come in with the *Laurentian* and warming frozen hands and feet on the hot-water registers in the station; watching a late-running *Canadian* buck the drifts of a December blizzard on the last lap into Windsor Station, and being awestruck at the unforgettable sight of FP7 4066 and RS10 8560 struggling through coupler-deep snow with *The Atlantic Limited*. Best of all was being permitted past the wire ticket wickets, beyond the solid oak door marked Private, and into the sanctuary of the train order/ticket office on the February 1971 day that Stan was called to work the day-operator job at Montreal West.

The Kodachromes exposed on that snowy February day may someday fade. The memories

Putting on an unforgettable performance, Engineer Bill Griffin brings No. 41, *The Atlantic Limited,* into Montreal West, Quebec, with FP7 4066 and RS10 8560 plowing through drawbar-deep snow on December 28, 1969. *Stan J. Smaill*

will not. More than a quarter century has passed and Montreal West has changed dramatically; the tower has been closed and *The Atlantic Limited*, the *Laurentian*, the *Montreal Limited* are history and even *The Canadian* is gone. The station has been gutted and renovated in a style that better serves its function as a commuter stop, and most of the railroaders who worked there have retired. However, you can still sit in the Smaill kitchen, recall those memorable days and listen to FP7's howl in the distance as they accelerate commuter trains away from the station at Montreal West. It's comforting to know that after better than 25 years, some things haven't changed.

Struggling to keep the switches clean at the height of a blizzard, the section men at Montreal West take a break as CP 4074, 8597, 8780 and 4070 storm out of town with No. 41, *The Atlantic Limited*, on February 20, 1971. *Greg McDonnell*

Fresh from repairs, CP M630 4562 idles on the shop track at St. Luc, Quebec, while ailing sister 4551 awaits attention on September 4, 1991. *Greg McDonnell*

Reposing in the diesel shop at St. Luc, Quebec, CP M636 4703 receives "runthrough" service between assignments on July 10, 1991. *Greg McDonnell*

Instruments of last resort, a pipe wrench, hammer and baling wire hang on a blackened hood door of CP M630 4566 at St. Luc, Quebec, on September 4, 1991. Work orders written against the aging M-line reveal a host of mechanical ailments, but there is still life to be wrung from the oil-stained Alco 16-251 engine under its hood. Shop crews will soon have the unit back on the road and the elderly freighter will put in a few more months and a few thousand revenue miles before bad-order liners and excessive vibration permanently sideline the big Alco on January 11, 1992. *Greg McDonnell*

The sun is setting on steam operations throughout North America, but sunrise on a June 1959 morning finds CP G3-class Pacifics 2461, 2426 and 2412 under steam at Vaudreuil, Quebec, ready to wheel commuters to Windsor Station in downtown Montreal. *Paul Meyer*

Wearing the gaudy paint of their new owner, the Montreal Urban Community Transportation Corporation, former-CP FP7's 1305, 1304 and 1301 (ex-CP 4075, 4074 and 4071) strike a similar pose at Vaudreuil on October 25, 1986. Like the Pacifics they replaced, the venerable cabs are remarkable for their longevity—if not their looks. In 1996, the Montreal commuter authority's five ex-CP FP7's are among the last of their kind in regular service anywhere. *Greg McDonnell*

True to its pool train designation, CN No. 9 has a single CP express car in its consist as FP9 6501 brings the Belleville–Toronto maid-of-all-work into Port Hope, Ontario, on May 11, 1962. *James A. Brown*

Night mail. Operating in the grand tradition of overnight mail and express trains, CN FPA4 6779, RS18 3113 and GP9 4101 accelerate Toronto–Montreal express train No. 250 out of Mimico Yard at 2018, June 5, 1978. After pausing at Bathurst Street to lift mail and express loaded at the downtown post office and freight sheds, No. 250's engineer will put the high-speed gearing of his passenger-assigned locomotives to good use. *Greg McDonnell*

On Her Majesty's Service

With a smart rap, the cancelling hammer struck the letter bill and left its circular mark: MONT. & TOR. R.P.O. 59 24 AP 71 NO. 11. At a heavily scarred and ink-stained desk in a bouncing, swaying RPO car, the clerk continued, deftly alternating the hammer between the ink pad and the stack of pink letter bills, imprinting each with the Montreal & Toronto Railway Post Office cancellation mark as CN train 59 hurtled through the night. While passengers aboard the Montreal–Toronto overnighter slept, Railway Mail Service clerks aboard the RPO car on the head end of the train performed a rite almost as old as railroading—sorting and processing the Royal Mail in transit.

The close relationship between the Post Office Department and the passenger train can be traced to the very earliest days of Canadian railroading. Indeed, as early as 1840, the Champlain & St. Lawrence, the nation's first railway, earned the sum of 52 pounds sterling for the carriage of closed mailbags aboard its daily passenger train. In 1851, the General Railroad Act mandated that the railroads carry mail subject to the demands of the Postmaster General. By 1854, postal clerks were sorting mail aboard the country's first Railway Post Office cars. For the next century, RPO cars were fixtures on hundreds of the country's passenger trains, from transcontinental flagships to lowly locals and mixed trains.

Canada's Railway Mail Service reached its pinnacle in 1950, the year that 1,385 RMS clerks racked up 22,489,547 revenue miles working 192 RPO runs nationwide. Competition on the highways and in the air soon took its toll, though, and one by one railway mail contracts were cancelled. Twenty-one years later, Canada had but three surviving Railway Post Office runs: Campbellton & Levis on CN trains 122/123; Ottawa & Toronto on CN trains 48/49 and Montreal & Toronto on CN trains 58/59.

On April 24, 1971, 117 years of history and tradition came to an end as the remaining RPO's made their final runs. Dignitaries and railway officials attended ceremonies at Levis, Quebec, as CN No. 123 pulled in with the Cam. & Levis RPO, the last Railway Post Office to operate in Canada. Hours earlier, the Ottawa–Toronto and Montreal–

In the gloomy confines of the train shed at Toronto Union Station, baggage carts are piled high with mail waiting to be loaded aboard a CN RPO car in the summer of 1957. *James A. Brown*

Toronto RPO's passed into history, attracting little more than local attention. However, as the Montreal & Toronto RPO on CN No. 59 neared the end of its run, one of the clerks grabbed a stack of surplus letter bills and banged out a series of last-day cancellations as a favor for a postal supervisor's son. That simple gesture said more than any rehearsed tribute or prepared media statement.

A decade after the last Railway Post Office runs were terminated, the low autumn sun plays upon the rivetted sides of a derelict CN RPO car. Still attired in pre-1960 green and black, Mail & Express car 7819 recalls a time when red Royal Mail trucks met every train and letters could be posted on the station platform—or through the

Mail handlers at Toronto Union Station unload CN 8041, one of four baggage cars of mail that arrived on Montreal–Toronto No. 59 on June 5, 1978. While RPO's were long gone, a number of CN passenger trains continued to carry mail in sealed baggage cars. *Greg McDonnell*

Bearing the scratches and scars of uncounted tens of thousands of mail bags picked up on the fly, or heaved aboard from baggage carts and mail trucks, CN RPO 7819 (carrying OCS number 73924) awaits its fate at the Spadina Coach Yard in Toronto on October 20, 1981. *Greg McDonnell*

slot in the side of the RPO car. Scratches and chipped paint surrounding the old catch-arm brackets bear testament to hundreds of mail pouches picked up on the fly, while the doorways wear the scars inflicted by uncounted tens of thousands of mailbags heaved aboard the car from baggage carts and waiting trucks.

Through grated windows and broken glass, sunlight probes the musty interior of the car, and an unlocked wooden door offers passage into a once forbidden place restricted to "the exclusive accommodation of the Mails and the persons specially appointed to take charge of the same." Walls of dusty sorting cases and racks of rust-encrusted hooks waiting for mailbags that will never come conjure visions of clerks busily sorting

30 to 40 letters per minute, and mail handlers wrestling heavy bags laden with Eaton's and Simpson's catalogues, bundles of *Maclean*'s and *Saturday Night* and rolled-up copies of the *Globe and Mail*. In the gloomy shadows of the condemned car, you can almost hear the low conversation of hurried clerks, the rustling of bags being emptied and the thump of cancelling hammers. Though the 7819's days are numbered, the legacy of the Railway Post Office will live on in memories, photographs and, thanks to the considerate act of an unknown clerk, a set of last-day cancellations from the MONT. & TOR. R.P.O.

Facing the Wrecking Ball

Like a fiery rain, sparks and molten metal showered into the darkened stalls as wrecking crews on the roundhouse roof cut through smoke jacks and overhead steelwork. Time had finally caught up with CN's Spadina roundhouse, a Toronto landmark that had stood at the foot of its namesake street for more than 60 years. Spadina had serviced its last locomotive, the shops were empty and the last workers had checked out, leaving little more than memories and the lingering aroma of grease, oil and sweat. Soon, even that would be gone. Several stalls away, a giant backhoe clawed at the brickwork, smoke-blackened timbers creaked their last, and the walls of one of the most famous roundhouses in Canada came tumbling down.

Opened in 1927, Spadina, located several blocks west of Toronto Union Station, stabled some of CN's premier passenger power, from high-drivered K-5-a Hudsons to streamlined 6400-series Northerns. However, Spadina's greatest claim to fame was its accessibility. The Spadina Avenue overpass that spanned the busy Toronto Terminals trackage approaching Union also crossed the shop leads and service tracks leading to the 36-stall roundhouse. The massive concrete-and-steel structure may have been created to carry vehicular and pedestrian traffic across the railway, but it also served a higher purpose. The Spadina overpass was not only one of the finest train-watching locations in the city, it was a public observation platform overlooking one of the busiest round-houses in the nation.

Leaning on the iron railings of the great bridge, generations of train-watchers learned the intimacies of lubricating Walschaerts and Baker

A shower of sparks rains to the floor of a darkened stall in CN's Spadina roundhouse as crews demolish the Toronto landmark on May 8, 1986. *Greg McDonnell*

valve gear, the art of "oiling around" and the unpleasantries of working the ash pits. Inhaling coal smoke and standing amid the roar of open pops and blowers, thumping air pumps and whining turbogenerators, they studied every detail of the engines crowding the shop tracks below, from pre-nationalization 0-6-0's and Pacifics, to bullet-nosed Mountains and handsome Northerns.

Dieselization did not doom Spadina. As steam bowed out, the water tower and standpipes were removed and the ash pits filled in, but the massive concrete coal tower and sanding plant remained in place and Spadina went about the business of servicing and repairing diesels with little physical change. In stalls that once berthed Pacifics, Hudsons and Northerns, workers tended to the ailments of F-units and Alco-design cabs, C-lines and S-series switchers. Fuel racks were installed near the coal tower and high-level service stands were erected, but the view from the Spadina overpass, looking

Framed in the doors of the roundhouse, VIA FPA4 6762 and CN S13 8522 slumber on the turntable leads at Spadina on June 28, 1985. *Greg McDonnell*

across shop leads filled with idling FPA4's and FP9's, Geeps, RS18's and S2's, was as captivating as ever.

Near the south end of the overpass, an iron stairway led from the bridge to track level. Night or day, the faithful were free to descend those stairs and, upon signing a release, explore the roundhouse and shop tracks at will. While access to many shops changed with the policies of the division superintendent, or the mood of the shop foreman on duty, Spadina's consistent hospitality and friendly atmosphere made it unique among big-city roundhouses.

Although Spadina survived dieselization, as well as the 1978 VIA takeover of passenger operations, the venerable facility could not withstand the pressures to redevelop Toronto's prized railway lands. In 1985, the Spadina site was selected as the location for a domed stadium to be built for the American League Toronto Blue Jays. VIA vacated the roundhouse and adjacent coach yards that fall, and the demolition orders were signed. As Spadina faced the wrecking ball, plans for the new SkyDome were finalized and "Home of the Dome" graffiti appeared on the walls of the doomed roundhouse.

As one whose formative years included hundreds of hours under Spadina's tutelage, I was bound to pay last respects to the place. On May 8, 1986, nearly 30 years after my first visit, I

slipped past the wrecking crews and took a final walk through the skeletal remains of the partially demolished roundhouse. Just hours ahead of the wreckers, I moved cautiously through the dark empty stalls recalling a lifetime of Spadina experiences, from childhood glimpses of steam engines lined up on the ready tracks, to hours spent examining engines at rest or under repair in the crowded, dimly-lit stalls; taking the throttle of an aging S2 on the service track and riding the cab of Northern 6218 as hostlers put her to bed after an autumn excursion; sharing beans with engine crews in the bunkhouse kitchen and checking the engine assignment board to discover a back-to-back set of FPA4's chalked up for No. 151 and the cab ride home.

There was a certain sadness about the occasion, but an even greater sense of satisfaction as I reflected upon the lessons learned within the curved, smoke-stained walls of the dingy roundhouse. In the course of our long association, Spadina had enriched my railroad experiences and instilled a lasting respect for the hard-working labourers, machinists and mechanics who toiled unnoticed behind shop walls and roundhouse doors. With a sickening crash, the brick walls of a nearby stall succumbed to the blows of a powerful backhoe, putting an end to my meditation. As the wreckers slowly advanced, I walked away from the ruins, knowing that Spadina had given me something that the wrecking ball could never destroy.

While FP9's 6515 and 6517 peer from their stalls, CN U-1-f Mountain 6076 eases onto the turntable at Spadina in the pouring rain on July 4, 1958. *J. Parker Lamb*

Silhouetted in swirling steam and the low morning sun, an ancient CN 0-6-0 shuffles along Toronto Terminals Railway trackage at Bathurst Street on February 19, 1954. *Robert Sandusky*

Racing along the lakeshore in west-end Toronto, CN RS3 3040 and RS18 3639 rattle through Sunnyside with a short eastbound freight headed for Mimico Yard in September 1963. Mimico was CN's main yard in Toronto until the opening of Toronto Yard (now MacMillan Yard) in 1965. *Matthew J. Herson, Jr.*

Her freshly wiped face glistening in the low afternoon sun, beetle-browed CN Northern 6143 eases past a set of
Wabash F7A's on the shop track at Fort Erie, Ontario, in July 1958. *James Van Brocklin*

Showing off her one-of-a-kind number plate, CN U-2-h 4-8-4 6258, one of the last Northerns acquired by the railway, moves down the shop lead at Fort Erie, Ontario, in July 1958. *James Van Brocklin*

Nearly 30 years later, CN HR616 2101, two M636's and GP9 4209 idle outside the Fort Erie shop on August 19, 1987. While neither her looks nor builder's plates offer any clues, Bombardier-built 2101 is one of the last locomotives CN acquired from the Montreal works that constructed both the 6143 and 6258. *Greg McDonnell*

The Greatest Show on Earth

Elephants trumpet and shuffle about anxiously as roustabouts, with bales of hay hoisted on their shoulders, arrive with dinner. Off-duty performers, acrobats, trainers and unmasked clowns pace impatiently, smoking cigarettes and taking swigs from cans of Budweiser, while the trainmaster barks into a cellular phone and the fearsome growl of lions and tigers sends chills down the spine. Standing on the sidelines, a young boy, tightly gripping his father's hand, looks on in wonder. The circus is in town.

On a rainy October 1994 afternoon, the Ringling Bros. and Barnum & Bailey circus train has paused at CP's Montrose Yard in Niagara Falls, Ontario, to clear Customs and allow feeding and watering of the animals on board. With the circus booked for a four-day stand in Toronto, the train will not linger, but the short stop affords outsiders a rare opportunity to step behind the curtains of the Big Top. While Customs officials inspect the train, the few onlookers witness the unrehearsed antics of the elephants (playfully teasing their handlers and pulling baggage car doors shut with their trunks), and in brief conversations with performers and workers, gain a tantalizing peek at the mystical world of circus life. For those gathered at Montrose, it's the equivalent of a backstage pass.

The days of open flats loaded with brightly painted circus wagons are gone, but the circus train is still the closest that thousands of small-town and rural residents will ever get to the Big Top. Led by CP Rail SD40-2's 5550 and 5478, the Ringling Bros. and Barnum & Bailey "Red Unit," a 53-car train made up of streamlined passenger equipment converted to animal cars and dormitories, private cars, generator, office and tool cars, several 89-foot piggyback flats loaded with trucks, trailers and containers, and a single bi-level auto rack, is every bit the worthy heir of the grand circus trains of old. The circus may open in Toronto on Thursday, but tonight, as the two SD's hurtle the silvered train through vineyards and villages along the Niagara Escarpment, through the back streets of Hamilton and past lakeshore suburbs, its passage will quicken the pulse and provide an unforgettable thrill to children of all ages. Don't tell P.T. Barnum, but that just might be the greatest show on Earth.

Grinding up the Niagara Escarpment, CP SD40-2's 5820 and 5798 roll the 53-car, 3720-ton Ringling Bros. and Barnum & Bailey Circus train through Vinemount, Ontario, at 1120, November 7, 1994. In just over 24 hours, the circus is scheduled to play in Pittsburgh. *Greg McDonnell*

As a young family looks on, roustabouts feed and water the elephants as "The Greatest Show on Earth" pauses at CP's ex-NYC Montrose Yard in Niagara Falls, Ontario, on October 31, 1994. The elephant in car 67 is using his trunk to close the baggage car door. *Greg McDonnell*

Flying freshly laundered flags, CN U-2-h Northern 6240 stomps out of Kitchener, Ontario, after meeting an eastbound passenger train (visible making its station stop) on an August 1958 evening. *Paul Meyer*

Framed in the window of the Station Hotel, VIA FPA4 6763 pauses at Kitchener, Ontario, with Sarnia-bound No. 83 at 1510, August 19, 1987. Looking back from the cab of the vintage MLW, the fireman, anxious to get a breeze blowing through the non-airconditioned cab, impatiently awaits a highball on the hot afternoon. *Greg McDonnell*

Grand River Railway Baldwin-Westinghouse steeplecab No. 230 (ex-Salt Lake & Utah 106) waits in the wings as CP P2g Mikado 5405, a helper engine returning from Orr's Lake, takes the siding at Galt, Ontario, on a September 1959 morning. Although both the Baldwin motor and the MLW-built Mike are on borrowed time, the electric will fare better. After the Preston-based CP Electric Lines were dieselized in October 1961, the 230 was sold to the Cornwall Street Railway, where it survived on the Cornwall, Ontario, switching road as No. 17 until that line was acquired by CN and dieselized in 1971. Retired in October 1971, No. 17 was preserved and put on display at Cornwall. Cut up for scrap in the spring of 1965, the 5405 gained notoriety as one of the last CPR steam locomotives to be scrapped. *James Van Brocklin*

Baldwin steeplecabs, catenary and steam helpers are long gone, but the trains continue to roll through Galt. Taking advantage of a recent ice storm, neighbourhood boys play a game of pick-up hockey as No. 50, with SD40's CP 5549 and QNS&L 211, passes at 1222, January 4, 1985. *Greg McDonnell*

Even the begrimed flanks of CN C630M 2030, HR616 2108 and SD40-2 5264 take on a golden glow in the setting sun as eastbound hotshot
No. 392 slams through Princeton, Ontario, at 1726, February 7, 1987. *William D. Miller*

Amid the brilliant colours of an autumn afternoon, CP M636 4708, M630 4557 and M636 4732 tackle Orr's Lake Hill with No. 925's freight at 1324, October 13, 1989. *Greg McDonnell*

Lake Effects and Legends

Hang on!" Brad Jolliffe shouts across the cupola. "This is going to be rough." Before the words are out, the battered Russel-built wedge plow slices into the heavy drift and begins to rock, shake and bounce violently. An explosion of snow swallows the plow and a barrage of frozen chunks pound against the cupola windows. Visibility is nil and speed is dropping rapidly as Jolliffe squeezes the transmit key on the radio mike and tells the hogger to give it all he's got. Back in the cab of Goderich–Exeter GP9 180, Tom Jackson widens the throttle to Run 8, but the aged Geep's 1750 horsepower is no match for the heavy drifts. Within a train length, GEXR Plow Extra 180 East is stalled in the frame-deep snow east of Mitchell, Ontario.

With a loud rush of air, the plow's wings retract and bang tightly against the carbody to allow the train to back clear of the drift. However, the 180 will not make the transition to reverse until Jackson, with water from melting snow dripping off the cab ceiling and running down the electrical cabinet walls, manipulates the relays by hand. Had the risky procedure failed, the Plow Extra would have been stranded as drifting snow quickly filled in the cut behind the train—a situation with which Jolliffe and Jackson are all too familiar.

Nervously eyeing the air gauges—and watching the pressure slowly drop as the train line freezes—Jolliffe gives the highball to attack the drift a second time. With a half-mile run, Plow Extra 180 East charges forward, and like a rough-riding rodeo bronc, the old Russel bucks and heaves, bounces

and bumps and breaks its way through. Victory comes at a price though, for the plow's air-reservoir pressure has dropped to 35 pounds and alarm bells are ringing aboard the 180 as the Extra grinds to a halt just clear of the drift. While Jackson cuts out a troublesome traction motor, Jolliffe drops to the ground, parts the air hoses between the engine and plow, and adds a measure of alcohol in an effort to thaw the frozen train line. Nearly a half hour will pass before the Plow Extra is able to resume the battle to reach Stratford.

Since coming on duty at Goderich at dawn, the crew have struggled to make 35 miles in 8 hours; the sun will have set by the time they make Stratford, just 46 miles from their starting point on the shore of Lake Huron. It will be near midnight when the train limps back in to Goderich with its weary crew, half-frozen plow and crippled GP9. By snowbelt standards, that's a good day.

Winter railroading in the Southern Ontario snowbelt, where lake-effect snows bring annual accumulations of over 100 inches and high winds pile hard-packed drifts 10 to 12 feet deep, is the stuff of legends. Seasoned veterans tell of plows flipping end over end; of snow smashing cab and cupola windows and burying crews inside; of trains stranded for days and even weeks; and of harrying trips and wild rides that could fill a book on their own.

With the abandonment of hundreds of miles of trackage in the lee of Lake Huron, snowbelt railroaders have become a vanishing breed. Indeed, the Goderich–Exeter crews working GEXR's former

CN Stratford–Goderich and Clinton Jct.–Centralia lines are among the last. However, as long as steel rails cross the squall lines and streamers that blow inland from Lake Huron each winter; as long as railroaders are up to the challenge of battling blinding snowstorms and headlight-high drifts—and brave enough to climb aboard ancient wedge plows for nerve-wracking, adrenalin-pumping, bone-rattling rides—the legend will remain alive.

Riding in the foreman's seat of Goderich–Exeter's ex-CN plow 55437, Brad Jolliffe prepares to do battle with the legendary Lake Huron snows aboard Plow Extra 180 East on February 13, 1994. *Greg McDonnell*

A welcome sight with his snow blower-equipped tractor, farmer John McGregor comes to the rescue of Goderich–Exeter GP9's 177, 180 and 179, hopelessly stuck in drifts as high as their cab windows, at Mileage 16.5, just east of Dublin, Ontario, on January 20, 1994. Until the arrival of McGregor, crewmen Brad Jolliffe and Tom Jackson spent hours attempting to dig out the stranded Geeps. In the winter of 1993–94, this was an all too common experience for beleaguered GEXR crews. *Brad Jolliffe*

With less than one year to live, CNR Ten-Wheelers 1564, 1560 and 1348 slumber in the roundhouse at Palmerston, Ontario, on August 1, 1958. *Alvin H. Brown*

Always Look Back

Striking a timeless pose, CNR Ten-Wheelers 1564, 1560 and 1348 quietly doze in the Palmerston, Ontario, roundhouse on August 8, 1958. The well-kept engines barely show their age, but all three predate the First World War. Recently renumbered H-6-g's 1560 and 1564 were outshopped from MLW in 1912 as Canadian Northern 1370 and 1374, while H-6-f 1348 (still carrying its original road number) was turned out by Baldwin in 1911 for CNoR subsidiary Duluth Winnipeg & Pacific. For a father and son on a 10-day search for steam, the elderly trio are a welcome sight, and roundhouse foreman Norman Dougall is only too happy to give the visitors, Al Brown and his son Jim, the royal treatment—including spinning 1564 on the turntable.

In the summer of 1958, steam is making a valiant last stand, but the railways' dieselization programs are in full swing. Steam has already been banished from entire divisions, and the books of the nation's locomotive builders are bulging with orders for cab units and road switchers that will finish the job. For the moment, at least, Palmerston, a busy branchline division point and the hub of CN's extensive network of Bruce Peninsula branches, remains a steam stronghold.

If the end is near, it is evident in neither Dougall's enthusiasm, nor the pride with which his men care for the ancient but well-maintained

Amid the last remains of recently scrapped engines, including J-7-b Pacific 5286, CN H 6 f 4 6-0 1348 meets its end at Reclamation in London, Ontario, on July 20, 1959. *James A. Brown*

Moguls, Ten-Wheelers and Pacifics assigned to the Palmerston roundhouse. However, even as Al Brown frames the classic trio in the viewfinder of his Rollei, a pair of the 1700-series RSC13's—the engines that will soon doom not only Palmerston's steam, but the roundhouse jobs and the shop itself—are idling on the ready track outside.

For Palmerston's pretty little engines, the end came swiftly. Less than a year later, the younger Brown encountered CN 1348 again, not under steam on some Bruce branch local, but at CN's Reclamation Yard on the east end of London,

Ontario. The smell of death, an acrid blend of acetylene and hot metal, hung heavy in the air as a lone worker, perched atop the carcass of the old Baldwin, methodically cut the engine apart. With a gut-wrenching groan, the smoke box split in two and crashed to the ground, already littered with pieces of the 1348, as well as the last remains of the engines that had gone before her. Brown dutifully recorded the moment, but the poignant photographs do more than document the end of a locomotive, they put the priceless images of Palmerston the previous summer in proper context.

Arriving from her namesake port on the Ohio side of Lake Erie, the Pennsylvania–Ontario Transportation Company car ferry *Ashtabula* churns up the water as she prepares to dock at the CPR slip at Port Burwell, Ontario, in July 1957. With locomotive coal as her staple traffic, the *Ashtabula's* fortunes were already low when the vintage boat, built by the Great Lakes Engineering Works in 1906, sunk in Ashtabula harbour after colliding with the freighter *Ben Moreell* on September 18, 1958. As a result, the last remaining Lake Erie car ferry service was abandoned. The *Ashtabula* was subsequently refloated and scrapped. *James Van Brocklin*

Sitting in the cab of his father's Chevy pickup, a young boy seems more intent upon the photographer than the homing pigeons being loaded aboard the combine of CP Port Burwell–Woodstock mixed No. 659, stopped at a crossing in Tillsonburg, Ontario, in July 1957.
James Van Brocklin

Utilizing a string of idler flats, CP D10j 986 reaches into the hold of the *Ashtabula* for a cut of coal hoppers.   *James Van Brocklin*

Reflected in the still waters of the Lynn River, Grand River Railway 864, bound for Port Dover as LE&N train No. 14, ambles across the low wooden trestle at Simcoe, Ontario, on April 24, 1955, the last day of passenger service on the CPR Electric Lines. *Robert Sandusky*

Threatening skies contrast with the peaceful water of the Speed River as the GRR "North Job," punctuated by wooden CP van 437142, passes through Preston, Ontario, at 0755, May 28, 1980. *Greg McDonnell*

Bound for Port Rowan and Port Dover, CN mixed train M233 makes its station stop at Caledonia, Ontario, while S-1-f Mikado 3422, heading up Brantford–Fort Erie mixed M218, takes water on an August 1957 morning. *James Van Brocklin*

En route to Port Dover with mixed train M238, CN E-10-a Mogul No. 83 satisfies her thirst at the imposing wooden tank at Lynn Valley, Ontario, on April 17, 1954. While seven of CN's ex-Grand Trunk E-10-a class Moguls were preserved, 83 was not. The dapper 2-6-0 was retired in 1959 and scrapped. *James Van Brocklin*

Leaning on the stock-pen gate, a farmer, with perhaps even more seniority than pre-First World War vintage CP 275738, supervises as workers unload stock cars at Waldemar, Ontario, on July 18, 1970. The Teeswater Sub., like many Southern Ontario branch lines, continued to receive cattle well into the 1970s. Shipments to pens located on CP main lines in Southern Ontario lasted until the late 1980s. *James A. Brown*

The seasonal rush of stock shipments from prairie ranches to Southern Ontario pastures was still an annual event in the early 1980s, as evidenced by the lengthy cut of stock cars on the head end of CP Extra 4744 West, racing into the sunset east of Galt, Ontario, at 1707, November 3, 1981. *Greg McDonnell*

The Price of Progress

Probing the darkness with its bright yellow light, the train-order signal, its blistered wooden blades silhouetted against the starry night sky, maintains its faithful vigil high above the CPR station at Guelph Jct., Ontario. In the operator's office below, bulletin orders hang ready on their hooks, blank train-order forms and clearances are arranged neatly on the desk, and swing operator Morley Janes waits patiently to copy train orders that will never come. The selector has hammered out its codes for the last time, the bells are stilled and a bulletin posted nearby notifies all concerned that train-order operation on the Galt Subdivision will cease at 2330, July 5, 1986. Effective 0001, July 6, 1986, train operations on the Galt Sub. will be governed by a radio-dispatched, computer-aided Manual Block System.

At 2330—on the dot—signal maintainer Jack Laking cuts the power to the signal and climbs the mast. Working by lamplight, he quickly unfastens the eastward semaphore signal and carefully lowers it to the ground on the end of a rope. At 2339, the westward semaphore gently hits the ground and the train-order era is history.

With the elimination of train-order dispatching, railroading lost more than a time-honoured art. The end of train-order operation was the kiss of death for many surviving stations and hundreds of operators' jobs. While the efficiencies of MBS are undeniable, the new order (redesignated OCS, "Operating Control System," with the introduction of the Canadian Rail Operating Rules in 1990) exacts its toll in the further dehumanization of railroading. For better or worse, the days of leaning on the counter and passing time with the local operator, listening to the rhythmic litany of train-order repeats and eavesdropping on the train phone, the days of meet orders, "19Y west, copy three," and the timeless ritual of hooping trains are forever gone.

Following the official discontinuance of train-order operations on CP's Galt Subdivision, signal maintainer Jack Laking begins dismantling the train-order signal at Guelph Jct., Ontario, on July 5, 1986. *Greg McDonnell*

After governing movements on CP's Galt Sub. for generations, the train order signals at Guelph Jct., Ontario, lie on the platform, signalling the end of an era at 2339, July 5, 1986. *Greg McDonnell*

The station cat is curled up in a chair and the Seth Thomas clock steadily ticks toward midnight as the CP operator at Streetsville, Ontario, listens in on the dispatcher's phone at 11:37 p.m., March 3, 1960. *Robert Sandusky*

Silhouetted by the evening sun, the engineer on a CN passenger extra strikes a classic pose at the throttle of U1b Mountain 6034, eastbound out of Sarnia, Ontario, in July 1957. *James Van Brocklin*

Working at the desk of his assigned wooden van, CP 437238, Electric Lines conductor Bruce Gowing attends to paperwork at Kitchener, Ontario, on March 30, 1978. *Brad Jolliffe*

The archetypal passenger-service conductor, Mel Humble leans from the Dutch door of a coach on his train, CN Sarnia–Stratford–Toronto local No. 154, ready to depart Kitchener, Ontario, in November 1971. *Greg McDonnell*

Exiting Conrail's Canada Southern main for home-road rails, (via former L&PS trackage) Canadian-built C&O GP7's 5735 and 5736 lead Buffalo–Detroit freight CG-41 past the semaphore signals at BX Tower in St. Thomas, Ontario, at 1803, December 29, 1981. *Greg McDonnell*

Shadows highlight the ornate woodwork on C&O's ex-Pere Marquette depot at West Lorne, Ontario, still an open agency and train-order office on December 27, 1975. *Jeff Mast*

It's spring in Muskoka, and the green-and-gold garb of CN RS18 3833 accents the lush foliage as Extra 3833 South cruises through the rock cuts at Rosseau Road, Ontario, on June 1, 1962. *James A. Brown*

Dressed in fresh tuscan and grey paint, and proudly carrying the passenger–service beaver crest on her hood, CP RS10 8572 flies through Kleinburg, Ontario, with the Toronto section of the *Expo Limited* on June 4, 1967. Operated only during Centennial year, the Montreal–Vancouver *Expo Limited*, along with its connecting Toronto–Sudbury section, revived the schedule of the recently discontinued *Dominion*, along with many of the sleepers and dining cars mothballed with the demise of Nos. 7 and 8. For the heavyweight A-series dining cars, heavyweight R–, S– and T–class sleepers, as well as the streamlined Grove-series sleepers, the *Expo Limited*, discontinued on October 28, 1967, was the last hurrah. *James A. Brown*

In the great summer tradition of Southern Ontario stations, the Canadian National Exhibition poster is on prominent display as CP FA1 4007 and RS18 8788 slam past the depot at Parry Sound, Ontario, with a southbound time freight on August 15, 1964. *James A. Brown*

On a Sudbury Saturday night, the palpitating beat of Alco 244's fills the cold air as CP RS10 8475 and RS3 8449 peer into the turntable pit on February 22, 1975. *Greg McDonnell*

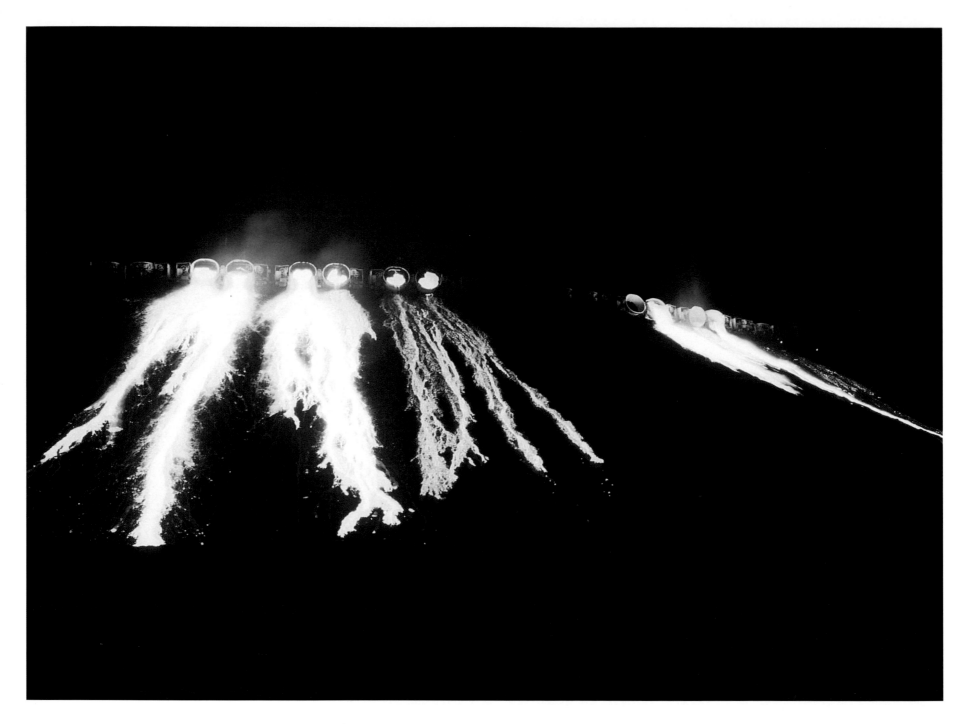

Illuminated by the fiery glow of molten slag, an Inco electric maintains a tight grip on its short train, while crews empty the slag pots, creating a spectacular light show at Sudbury, Ontario, on a warm August night in 1979. *Robert Sandusky*

In conditions of the opposite extreme, bitter cold, swirling steam, stainless steel and station lights combine to produce a similarly spectacular scene as VIA No. 1, the westbound *Canadian*, makes its stop at Sudbury on a frigid winter night. *Algonquin Park*, the first of CP's famed Budd-built Park cars, is carrying the markers of the transcontinental flagship on December 4, 1989. *Tom Lambrecht*

Leading Algoma Central No.16, the "Oba Turn," veteran GP7 152, drifts past the general store at Oba, Ontario, on February 22, 1976. *Greg McDonnell*

Sporting freshly applied Wisconsin Central crests and new road numbers, Algoma Central SD40-2 6005 and a pair of GP38-2's twist through the S-curves and rock east of Wawa, Ontario, with the "Harbour Job," on February 2, 1995, two days after WC took over the ACR. *Steve Glischinski*

Probing the fog rolling in off Superior's Peninsula Bay, CP Extra 5785 East approaches the Mink Tunnel on the edge of Mink Harbour on September 19, 1985.
John F. Garden

Superior

A billowing fog rolls in off Peninsula Bay and the cold black waters of Lake Superior, driven by a chilling wind, crash against the rocks at Mink Harbour. Hard between the ominous waters of the great inland sea and the jagged cliffs that rise from the water's edge, CP Rail's Heron Bay Subdivision clings to a narrow ledge carved into the rock. More than a century after the fact, the feats of the hard-working, hard-drinking navvies who scratched this remarkable stretch of railway through terrain that Van Horne called "two hundred miles of engineering impossibilities" are awe inspiring. So too is the railroading, conducted in territory where slide fences and freshly dumped rip-rap bear testimony to the fact that even after a hundred years nature can reclaim the right of way on a whim.

From out of the fog comes the drone of labouring 645's and a headlight materializes in the mist. Trailing a mile of manifest freight, CP Extra 5785 East carefully traces the shoreline under the watchful eye of the brooding lake. Superior is placid on this September day, but within weeks, the mood of the lake will change dramatically. With the approaching winter, come the legendary gales of November, followed by blizzards and bone-chilling cold, as Superior vents all of its wrath on one of the most spectacular pieces of railroad in the land.

Just about to duck into the Mink Tunnel on February 1, 1976, CP 1411, 4477 and 1405 roll train No. 1, the westbound *Canadian*, through one of Superior's many winter storms. *Greg McDonnell*

The mercury has plunged below minus 35 degrees and wind-chill warnings are being broadcast on the radio as VIA's transcontinental flagships, *The Canadian and Super Continental*, pose side by side at Winnipeg, Manitoba, on February 1, 1981. Still operating on CP lines with former CP equipment, *The Canadian* is headed up by ex-CP FP7 1403, along with boiler-equipped CP RS10's 8463, 8560 and GP9 8511, while the *"Super"* is in the charge of ex-CN FP9 6501 and an F9B. *Greg McDonnell*

Steam hangs heavy in the bitterly cold air as CN U-1-a Mountain 6000 simmers on the ready track at Fort Rouge, Manitoba, on January 25, 1959. *H.R. Clarke*

Bound for BN territory with Winnipeg–Noyes, Minnesota, No. 532, freshly overhauled CN F7Au 9165, GP9's 4322 and 4120 kick up the snow passing the old church at Union Point, Manitoba, at 1415, February 1, 1981. When the simple frame chapel was completed in 1887, the trains rolling through the churchyard were those of the Northern Pacific Railway. *Greg McDonnell*

Old Soldiers

Languishing on the deadline behind CN's Transcona shops, GP7 4809 sits derelict in the weeds. A veteran of the very earliest campaigns of dieselization, the venerable GP7—outshopped from GMD London as CN 7564 in October 1953—was among CN's first road switchers and a member of the vanguard GP order that eventually sired a fleet of some 470 first-generation Geeps on the roster of the government road. Downgraded to transfer duty after racking up several million miles in road service, the aged warrior met its end in a low-speed collision in PGE's North Vancouver Yard in 1971. While the injuries were far from fatal, they were enough to warrant retirement of the vintage hood. Ironically, the very universality that made the 4809 and its kind so successful made the crippled Geep worth more as a parts source than a rebuild candidate.

Along with a handful of retired F-units, a couple of wrecked GP9's and a few other survivors of CN's original GP7 order, the 4809 spends its final days in the back lot of Transcona, the very shop that maintained the unit and performed most—if not all—of its heavy overhauls. Still dressed in the green and gold of the glory days, CN 4809 has rolled its last mile. Gradually surrendering reusable engine and electrical components, body parts and even window glass, another old soldier slowly fades away.

Long retired, CN GP7 4809, still dressed in the classic green and gold of her prime, languishes on the scrap line behind Transcona shops on July 15, 1980. *Greg McDonnell*

Wheeling empty grain boxes of all sizes, CP G3h Pacific 2446 storms into Portage la Prairie with an Extra West on a July 1959 evening. *Paul Meyer*

Converted to burn oil and relieved
of her conical "bullet nose,"
CN U-1-f Mountain 6067 stomps
out of Portage la Prairie, Manitoba,
with an 89-car Extra West bound
for Dauphin at 4:35 p.m.,
June 7, 1959.
Robert R. Malinoski

In terrain not readily associated with the prairies, CN No. 358, led by SD60F 5540, Dash 8-40CM 2447 and SD40's 5026 and 5049, curves through thick forest and swampy wetlands at Mileage 70 on the Togo Sub., near Deepdale, Manitoba, on September 24, 1993. *Mark Perry*

Rolling out of a spectacular prairie sunset, CN SD40 5223 and SD40-2 5273 hurtle through Dutton, Manitoba, with No. 358 on September 9, 1993. Silhouetted in the cab of the aging SD, crewmen L. Sulatyski and M. Wakula are homeward bound on the eastward time freight. *Mark Perry*

El Dorado!

E l Dorado. Inspired by the mythical city of fabulous treasures sought by sixteenth-century Spanish explorers, the word has come to be associated with any place of great wealth or opportunity. According to VIA Rail Canada, *Eldorado* is defined as car number 1159, one of 52 4-Section/4-Double Bedroom/8-Duplex Roomette E-series sleepers built by Pullman-Standard for CN in 1954. On January 29, 1981, the word and the car are one in the same. Tied to the tail end of VIA/CN train No. 92, the Churchill–Winnipeg *Hudson Bay*, the sleeping car *Eldorado* is indeed a place of fabulous wealth and opportunity.

Unlike its mythical namesake, VIA *Eldorado's* wealth consists not of silver and gold, but of less tangible treasures. Rolling across the frozen tundra on a crystal clear January night, the riches of this *Eldorado* are measured in the breathtaking beauty of the Northern Lights, as viewed from an open Dutch door; in the delightful conversation and entertaining stories of sleeping-car porter J. R.

"Jimmy" Stevenson; in the simple pleasure of retiring to the steam-heated comfort of Bedroom D, sliding between crisp white sheets and pulling up warm woollen blankets marked with the traditional CN maple leaf crest; and in the soul-satisfying experience of drifting to sleep with the lazy chant of 567's and the lullaby rhythms of steel wheels riding jointed 100-pound rail.

VIA has retired sleeping car No. 1159, and the F-units and steam-heated equipment that once worked the Churchill trains have been replaced by F40's and electrically heated stainless-steel cars. In 1996, the future of these trains is threatened and the very existence of the remote Churchill line has been the subject of debate for decades. However, as long as the trains continue to run, a ticket aboard Nos. 92 and 93 offers passage to El Dorado.

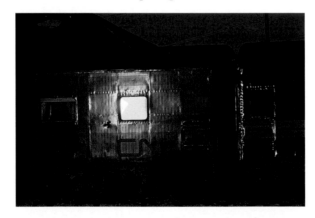

The setting Arctic sun plays on the flanks of CN sleeper *Eldorado* and freshly painted VIA diner 1346 as No. 92, the *Hudson Bay*, prepares to depart Churchill, Manitoba, on January 30, 1981. *Greg McDonnell*

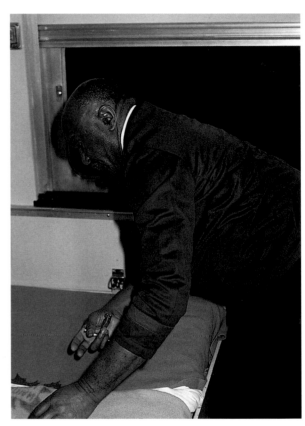

Somewhere south of Churchill, Manitoba, sleeping-car porter Jimmy Stevenson carefully prepares the bunk in Bedroom D of CN sleeper *Eldorado* as No. 92, the *Hudson Bay*, rolls across the frozen tundra on January 30, 1981. *Greg McDonnell*

Puncuated by an ancient wooden van and an even older steel combine, Churchill–Wabowden mixed No. 294 and No. 92, with the sleeper *Eldorado* on the tail end, weather an Arctic snowstorm at Churchill, Manitoba, on January 26, 1976. *Philip Mason*

After stopping to work the Manitoba Pool elevator at Jordan, Manitoba, CN GMD1's 1052 and 1070 get Miami/Hartney Sub. grain pickup 834 under way at 1228, July 24, 1980. *Greg McDonnell*

Ten-hundred Territory

Only units in series 1000-1076 permitted." The footnote, found in the Employee Timetable listings for dozens of CNR prairie branches, did more than establish trackage as the exclusive domain of CN's unique A1A-A1A GMD1's, it defined a branchline network little changed since the days of Canadian Northern 2-8-0's and outside-braced wooden boxcars.

Custom designed to replace pre-nationalization Ten-Wheelers, Pacifics and Consolidations on light-rail prairie branches, many laid with steel weighing as little as 56 pounds to the yard, CN's 6-axle GMD1's presided over a world seemingly frozen in time. Indeed, the arrival of the awkward-looking, but light-footed diesels did little more than eliminate the need for coal towers, water tanks and turntables. While the nation's railroads embraced CTC, 100-ton hoppers and Dash-2 diesels, time all but stood still in Ten-hundred territory. Oblivious to the affairs of the outside world, the A1A GMD1's carried on, towing strings of 40-foot boxcars over low-density grain branches, tiptoeing over wooden trestles, probing the weeds for 60-lb. rail milled before the turn of the century, and calling upon elevators in places named Amaranth, Avonlea and Elrose, Longburn, Lowe Farm and Livelong.

Throughout the sixties and seventies, abandonments and branch line rehabilitation programs slowly eroded the Ten-hundreds' light-rail empire. However, on July 24, 1980, the Miami Subdivision, a grain line tracing its ancestry to the Northern Pacific & Manitoba Railway, is one of a dozen southern Manitoba branches still restricted to Ten-hundreds only. Lifting out of Jordan after pausing to work the Manitoba Pool elevator, GMD1's 1052 and 1070 dig in, their A1A Flexicoil trucks clawing at 80-lb. rail in an effort to get the lengthy train of 40-foot grain boxes (with an old wooden stock car thrown in for good measure) up to the 25 mph track speed.

Rocking and rolling its way to the junction at Morris, Extra 1052 East is emblematic of the timelessness of railroading in Ten-hundred territory. Change, however, is on the horizon. By mid-decade, track gangs, rail and ballast trains will descend upon the Miami Sub., upgrading it to handle 100-ton hoppers and heavier diesels. In the process, the former Northern Pacific & Manitoba line will lose a measure of its charm, but will gain increased capacity and efficiencies that will ensure its survival.

Almost home, CN GMD1's 1003, 1011 and 1027 pass the semaphore guarding the diamond crossing CP's Carberry Sub. on the outskirts of Winnipeg, Manitoba, with No. 536, the Steep Rock wayfreight, at 1150, February 3, 1981. *Greg McDonnell*

Bucking drifts and battling high winds, CN GMD1's 1040 (still in the old green and gold) and 1060 work a Plow Extra on the Cudworth Sub. near Muskiki Springs, Saskatchewan, on February 20, 1979. *Andrew Sutherland*

Returning to Central Butte with loaded grain boxes, CN GMD1's 1012 and 1023 pass the abandoned ex-Grand Trunk Pacific station at Lawson, Saskatchewan, at 1625, September 30, 1976. *Andrew Sutherland*

Standing derelict on the empty prairie in the fall of 1976, the lonely CN station at Totzke, Saskatchewan, maintains its vigil at the junction of the Cudworth Subdivision, a former GTP branch to Prince Albert, and the Aberdeen Subdivision, once part of the Canadian Northern mainline. *Doug Phillips*

With a long cut of hoppers ahead of the hot piggyback traffic on "speed" No. 215, CN F7Au's 9163, 9159 and 9169 pass the elevators at Vanscoy, Saskatchewan, on May 11, 1987. *Robert J. Gallagher*

Utilitarian machines meet on the prairie as Northern Alberta Railways mixed No. 75, with GMD1's 302, 303 and 312, passes
a battered old Mercury pickup truck on the road near Callaghan, Alberta, on June 29, 1975. *Doug Phillips*

Mail, unloaded from the SOO Line RPO on No. 14, is piled higher than the cab of the mailman's pickup as the eastbound *SOO–Dominion*, with steam generator-equipped CP Train Master 8901, SOO RPO and baggage cars and a single CP 2200-series coach, conducts its business at Weyburn, Saskatchewan, on May 22, 1960. One of four CP H24-66 Train Masters delivered with full-width short hoods and dual steam generators, 8901 was regularly assigned to the *SOO–Dominion* and other secondary passenger runs on the Prairies. Bumped from their dual-service roles by the early 1960s, all four units (CP 8901-8904) surrendered their boilers and received standard short hoods. No. 8901 finished its career in Montreal transfer service and was scrapped after retirement in April 1972. Sister 8905 is preserved at the Canadian Railway Museum in Delson, Quebec, and is the only Train Master in existence. *Robert Sandusky*

Assigned to the hottest train on the road, 19-month-old CP GP30's 8201 and 8200, in the company of veteran FP7 4039, approach Indian Head, Saskatchewan, with transcontinental hotshot No. 901 on October 22, 1964. While the GP30 sold well in the United States, CP's pair, renumbered 5000–5001 in 1965, were the only Canadian ones built. *James A. Brown*

Van Horne's Wheat

Raise less hell and more wheat!" Van Horne's indignant response to the complaints of prairie farmers certainly made no new friends for the railway. But then, what damage could be done to a relationship with a group whose anthem, satirists claimed, was "God damn the CPR!" Whatever the farmers thought of Van Horne, though, they took his admonition to heart. Canada soon ranked as one of the world's largest producers and exporters of grain, much of which moved to market aboard the trains of the CPR.

At left: More wheat! CP grain train 355-134 charges across the prairie west of Brooks, Alberta, with SD40F-2 9020, SD40-2's 5943, 6026 and mid-train remotes 5708 and 6005 providing 15,000 hp to move the 120-car, 14,000-ton train to the Pacific tidewater. *Greg McDonnell*

From the Crow Rate to car shortages and subsidy disputes, grain transportation has been embroiled in politics and controversy since the first sack of wheat was heaved aboard a CPR boxcar in 1883. One hundred and thirteen years later, the debates rage on, from Parliament Hill and provincial legislatures, to the locals' table at Gibson's Restaurant in Gull Lake, Saskatchewan. All the while, a never-ending procession of grain trains have continued to rumble from prairie elevators to lakehead and tidewater ports.

On a peaceful Sunday morning in October 1995, the politics and economic arguments of the grain trade seem worlds away as CP Extra 9020 West thunders across the prairie with a 14,000-ton train of export wheat. The turbocharged howl of V16 645's shatters the Sabbath day solitude as SD40F-2 9020 and SD40-2's 5943 and 6026 grind past. Welded rail sings out and the ground quakes as loaded 100-ton hoppers rumble by. "Save the Crow" messages chalked in vain on the sides of bright red Trudeau hoppers and Tory-blue Heritage Fund cars emblazoned with state-applied graffiti ("Take an Alberta Break...visit Edmonton") conjure visions of Van Horne and the renegade farmers.

"More wheat!" he said, but the old man could never imagine annual harvests measured in tens of millions of metric tonnes, nor the endless parades of 120-car unit trains moving the grain to market. The tables have turned and here on the prairie west of Brooks, Alberta, the CPR is the one raising hell as Extra 9020 West follows the iron road to the Pacific with more wheat than even Van Horne dreamed possible.

A vanishing symbol of the Canadian prairies, the Saskatchewan Pool elevator at McMahon, Saskatchewan, glows in the afternoon sun on October 17, 1995. *Greg McDonnell*

Practising a nearly lost art, James Weiler loads CP 124087, a 40-foot, 40-year-old grain box with 2200 bushels of No. 2 Red Wheat at McMahon, Saskatchewan, on October 17, 1995. *Greg McDonnell*

Framed in the collapsing ruins of an abandoned farm, empty CP grain boxes rattle past a derelict Massey-Harris harvester at Vesper, Saskatchewan, at 1425, October 18, 1995.
Billed to the elevators at Simmie, the empty boxes are taking part in what will be the last harvest for the Dunelm Subdivision. *Greg McDonnell*

Plying the wobbly rails of the Notukeu Sub. (exaggerated by a heavy telephoto lens), CP GP38-2's 3032 and 3021 amble eastward with the Valmarie Turn on September 19, 1983. *John F. Garden*

Sun sets on the CP Notukeu Subdivision near Climax, Saskatchewan, on September 19, 1983. *John F. Garden*

Machinists tend to CP Royal Hudson 2849 while train No. 1 makes its station stop at Medicine Hat, Alberta, in the summer of 1953. Although No. 1 will change crews at the Alberta division point, the 2849 will work through to Calgary. As a regular passenger assignment, CP Hudsons worked Winnipeg–Calgary without change. *John Barras Walker*

Enjoying the view from the tender of CP T1a Selkirk 5905, the hostler takes a breather while the massive 2-10-4 slakes its 12,000-gallon thirst at the Medicine Hat, Alberta, roundhouse in October 1953. On the opposite track, T1c 5935 basks in the sun awaiting its next assignment. Bumped from their traditional mountain bailiwick by diesels, the legendary ten-coupled engines are finishing out their careers on the prairie. Delivered from MLW in March 1949, the 5935 was the last steam locomotive acquired by Canadian Pacific. In service for less than a decade, the engine was donated to the Canadian Railway Museum in Delson, Quebec. *John Barras Walker*

"It'd take a miracle to bring that old Fairbanks back." On June 19, 1974, workers at CP's Ogden Shops in Calgary, Alberta, are performing just such a miracle, repairing fire-damaged CPA16-4 4053. One of the last five surviving C-line cabs anywhere, 4053's good fortune was temporary. The CLC-built cab unit was retired a year later and scrapped. However, sisters 4065 and 4104 have been preserved. Former CLC demonstrator 4065 is at the Museum of Science and Technology at Ottawa, Ontario, while privately owned 4104 is in operable condition at the Museum of the Highwood Railway Project in High River, Alberta.
Greg McDonnell

Miracle at Ogden

Streaming through the grimy windows of CP's Ogden shop, rays of sunshine warm the battered carbody of CPA16-4 4053. Outshopped from the Canadian Locomotive Company's Kingston, Ontario, plant in July 1952, the aging C-line has seen better days. Her tuscan-and-grey paint is faded, her windshield layered in dust, and in the oily confines of her engine room, the lifeless opposed-piston engine bears evidence of a recent fire. Unlike the Geeps, SD's and F-units crowding the floor of the Calgary shop, 4053 came to Ogden to die.

Dead on arrival, CP 4053 joined the ranks of unserviceable CLC's on the Ogden scrap line after suffering a fire near Dalemead, Alberta, on April 19, 1974. Officially, the 4053 was listed as stored unserviceable, but fires and major component failures had felled dozens of her kind and there was little doubt that the venerable cab faced anything other than retirement. As it stood, 4053's withdrawal from service left sisters 4057, 4065, 4104 and 4105 as the last operating C-line cabs in existence. It would take a miracle to bring the 4053 back to life.

On June 19, 1974, that miracle has come to pass. The 4053 may have come to Ogden to die, but fate—and a worsening power shortage—have intervened. The aged Kingston-built cab has been lifted off its trucks and propped up on wooden blocks, roof sections have been removed and a blackened O-P engine peers from the carbody. With power tools, ladders and dollies laden with parts, workers clamber about, preparing the 1952-vintage CLC for reconditioned trucks, a rebuilt main generator and a miraculous return to service.

"Do not strip." The instructions chalked on the oil-smeared Fairbanks-Morse opposed-piston engine on the shop floor at Ogden give the promise of survival to at least one more CP CLC diesel in need of an engine change. In fact, no less than four O-P prime movers can be seen in the engine-rebuild area of the Calgary shop on May 17, 1972. *Doug Phillips*

Independence Day

I might even be intelligently argued that Canada's valid day of independence was November 7, 1885, for that was when the final spike on Canadian Pacific between Montreal and Vancouver was driven home at Craigellachie in Eagle Pass, B.C.

David P. Morgan, *Canadian Steam!*

One hundred and sixty-eight miles east of Craigellachie, snow falls softly on a lonely outpost high in the Rocky Mountains. Sullen clouds and blowing snow obscure the spectacular mountain peaks and a biting wind whips through stands of towering pines. Here at Divide, 5332 feet above sea level, just yards east of the Continental Divide and the entrance to Kicking Horse Pass, the air is thin, the skies are threatening and the mountains, locked in the grip of the merciless Canadian winter, seem unconquerable.

At the height of a January blizzard, this is a fearsome place. A place where nature's beauty and power are overwhelming. A place that puts into perspective the challenges that faced the railway builders over a century ago. A place that conjures visions of triple-headed Ten-Wheelers heading up varnished Limiteds; of double-shotted Decapods slogging upgrade with trains of 40-foot boxcars, and of Selkirks relaying tuscan heavyweights toward the Pacific. A place to consider Morgan's case for a Canadian independence day.

Amid the raging storm and the brooding peaks, the rails of Canadian Pacific's Laggan Subdivision slice the pristine snowscape like strands of silver inlay. Traffic on the nearby Trans-Canada Highway has ground almost to a halt, but the distant drone of labouring diesels announces the approach of a westbound freight—and delivers home the message that the CPR is neither slowed by the storm nor intimidated by the mountains.

The turbocharged thunder of General Motors 16-645E3 engines howls against the wind and a ghostly quartet of action-red SD's slowly emerge from the storm. Shrugging off the powdery snow, CP SD40-2's 5727, 5737, 5735 and veteran SD40 5501 grind toward the Great Divide with nearly a mile of loaded grain hoppers hung on their drawbars. The frozen earth quakes and snow gently swirls about as heavily burdened hundred-ton hoppers rumble westward. Tidewater-bound on a steel highway that stretches unbroken from the shores of the Atlantic to the Pacific coast, CP Extra 5727 West not only embodies the dreams of visionaries Howe, Macdonald and Fleming, Stephen, Van Horne and Rogers, it validates Morgan's suggestion that we celebrate the completion and continuing existence of the railway that defined and bound together the nation—and still does. On November 7th: Independence Day.

Endorsing David P. Morgan's case for a Canadian independence day, CP SD40-2's 5727, 5737, 5735 and veteran SD40 5501 shrug off the snow as they labour through Divide at 1110, January 24, 1990, tidewater bound on a steel highway that stretches unbroken from the shores of the Atlantic to the Pacific coast. *Greg McDonnell*

The chant of 567-series V16's rises above the sound of rushing waters as CP GP9's 8810 and 8832 grind up the Lower Kicking Horse Canyon through Glenogle, British Columbia, with No. 954 on September 20, 1970. A single action-red CP Rail boxcar in the consist of the eastbound freight heralds a new era on the "World's Greatest Travel System." *James A. Brown*

Approaching the Laurie snowsheds, CP SD40's 5535, 5543, 5538 and 5548 follow the course of the Illecillewaet River with an eastbound manifest on July 18, 1970. The eight-hatch reefers and the wood-sided, canvas-topped piggyback trailer on the train date the scene as surely as the tuscan-and-grey paint on the locomotives. *Matthew J. Herson, Jr.*

They may have traded their CP paint for VIA blue and yellow, but ex-CP FP7 1423, F9B 6652 and FP7 1418 are still performing their traditional duties, piloting VIA No. 1, *The Canadian*, through the Kicking Horse Pass west of Palliser, British Columbia, on February 11, 1982. *Brian Jennison*

In the minus 20 degree cold of an early-winter morning, mist from the Kicking Horse River shrouds CP SD40F-2 9013 and SD40-2 5934 as they depart Field, British Columbia, on a westbound drag on December 12, 1992. *Robert Sandusky*

CP FP7 1406, a boiler-equipped GP9 and another FP7 lead No. 2, the eastbound *Canadian*, near Cathedral, British Columbia, on August 12, 1978. *John F. Garden*

Exiting the tunnel at Cathedral, CP AC4400-CW's 9551 and 9548 claw their way toward the Spiral Tunnels with 992-11 at 1643, October 13, 1995. *Greg McDonnell*

As a summer storm sweeps across distant peaks, CN Extra 5116 West sprints across the Edson Sub., near Snaring, Alberta. Empty bulkhead flats and newsprint boxes en route to the BCR are light work for the pair of SD40's assigned to the westbound drag on July 18, 1986. *John C. Lucas*

Clinging to the mountainside near Gibbs, British Columbia, BC Rail M630's 719, 715, 716 and an M420B work northbound with Second 23 on July 20, 1986. *Dave Stanley*

Crossing the Fraser River at Lytton, British Columbia, CN SD40-2 5334 and five sisters wheel intermodal hotshot No. 218 eastward on August 11, 1981. *John F. Garden*

On June 1, 1991, CN GP40-2L's 9522 and 9437 roll autoracks along the shore of Brule Lake near Swan Landing, Alberta, in a setting the photographer describes as "the most spectacular location in all of the Rockies." *Richard Yaremko*

Slide Zone

While Yellowhead Pass afforded Canadian Northern the easiest of all rail crossings of the Continental Divide, Mackenzie and Mann's fledgling transcontinental paid the price when it reached the lower canyons of the Thompson and Fraser Rivers about 1914. Some thirty years earlier, the CPR had claimed the optimal route through the narrow confines of the treacherous canyons, leaving Canadian Northern the unenviable task of building a second railroad through some of the most forbidding terrain on

the continent. Construction costs on the "wrong side" of the canyons rose as high $300,000 per mile and eventually helped bankrupt the already troubled CNoR.

Notched into a near-vertical rock wall that soars almost a thousand feet above the seething waters of the Thompson River, CN's Ashcroft Subdivision clings to the side of the White Canyon east of Lasha, British Columbia. The perilous trackage bears testament to the challenges that confronted the builders of the Canadian Northern—and emptied the coffers of Mackenzie and Mann.

Viewed from the safety of the CPR side of the Thompson, CN Extra 5357 East carefully negotiates a spectacular and dangerous section of canyon

appropriately known as the Cape Horn slide zone. Slipping between two of seven tunnels in less than 15 miles, the transcontinental intermodal train is protected by slide-detector fences and three rock sheds constructed in deference to the frequent rock slides sent down the mountain as nature attempts to claw back the ledge carved out by the Canadian Northern.

Van Horne proclaimed the Fraser Canyon "one of the worst places in the world," but if he were looking for an equally tough place to build a railroad, he need only cast a glance across the Thompson at the Cape Horn slide zone.

At left: Ducking through the rock sheds, CN SD40-2 5357 and SD40's 5184 and 5167 pilot an eastbound hotshot through the Cape Horn slide zone along the Thompson River west of Lasha, British Columbia, on September 27, 1984. *Doug Phillips*

Headed for Crowsnest at 1505, February 20, 1974, Kootenay Division time freight No. 984 passes the old colliery at Michel, British Columbia, with an incredible collection of first-generation diesels. Led by CPA16-4 4057, the three-builder lashup includes CP H16-44 8715, F7B 4440 and FA2 4092, a rare visitor from the east. G.B. Will would approve. *John Sutherland*

With a wave to the head-end crew aboard CP H16-44 8728, operator Stan Smaill "PK's" the local as it departs Natal, British Columbia, at 0940, September 2, 1972. *John Sutherland*

For Engineer John Leeming and the crew of the CP Nakusp wayfreight on June 7, 1984, a bad day just got worse. Doubling the hill out of Nakusp, British Columbia, after stalling twice due to weeds and wet rail, GP9 8641 has turned a rail at Mileage 22.5 on the Kaslo Sub., bringing the day's work to an end. Tomorrow, crews from Nelson will employ air jacks, power tools and brute force to rerail the unit and restore the track. It will be dark before the train reaches Roseberry and the barge that will float it down Slocan Lake to Slocan City. *Brad Jolliffe*

On a better day, the tug *Iris G.* shepherds the Nakusp wayfreight, safely loaded aboard *Barge No. 6*, across Slocan Lake. Headed for the slip at Roseberry on August 8, 1978, the consist of the Nakusp job includes GP9 8640, a double-door boxcar, several empty pole-flats and assigned caboose 434125. *John F. Garden*

The booming exhaust of opposed-piston diesels echoes down the valley of the Kootenay River near Thrums, British Columbia, as CP CPA16-4 4064, CFB16-4 4455 and H16-44 8603 head west with Nelson–Tadanac freight No. 87 on October 20, 1964. Originally part of CLC's famed *City of Kingston* C-line demonstrator set, the 4064 (ex-CLC 7005) was scrapped in the early 1970s after suffering a serious fire in July 1969. Her *City of Kingston* partner, CP 4065 (ex-CLC 7006) has been preserved. As with all other CP H16-44's, the 8603 has been scrapped; however, CFB16-4 4455, converted to BCR Robot car RCC 3, has been earmarked for restoration and preservation, along with RCC 4, ex-CP 4456. *James A. Brown*

Still dressed in tuscan and grey, CP H16-44 8714 leads leased PNC GP9 166 (ex-QNS&L 166), GP9 8649 and H16-44's 8603 and 8710 on No. 87, following the Kootenay River west of Nelson, British Columbia, on June 24, 1974. *Greg McDonnell*

North Bend Beanery

"Canadian Pacific Spans the World." Etched in rust, the once-proud lettering and accompanying crest slowly reappear through layers of paint as rain streams down the sides of CP 240617, a derelict 1929-vintage boxcar parked in the deserted yard in North Bend, British Columbia. Standing alone on a weed-grown track, the lonely car recalls better times.

North Bend's days as a bustling division point are long past, but the tiny settlement remains a crew-change point and away-from-home terminal for CP Rail crews working trains on the Cascade and Thompson subdivisions. The station, round-house and turntable are gone and the CPR Hotel is no more than a memory, but a nondescript structure beside the main line beckons the weary traveller. Welcome to the "CP Rail North Bend Cafe."

On the outside, the CP Rail North Bend Cafe resembles an overgrown mobile home. On the inside, it's the classic railroad beanery, with well-worn stools along the counter and an open grill:

coffee brewing, hearty low-priced specials scrawled on the board (#1 T-bone $8.00) and a sign stencilled Booths Reserved for CP Employees. From train crews joking and flirting with the waitresses behind the counter, to tales of three o'clock calls and harrowing rides, the atmosphere is straight out of the pulp-fiction pages of *Railroad Magazine*.

Halfway through the best minestrone west of the Continental Divide, a bleary-eyed hogger with a 1300 call comes in from the pouring rain. His face speaks volumes on the rigours of railroading, of long hours, hard miles and sleep deprivation. Even before his eggs are flipped on the grill, the roadmaster's hi-rail truck pulls up outside; there's word of a rock fall in a tunnel west of town and another trip goes bad. If Harry Bedwell were here, he'd have another story.

Rain drips from a battered switch stand at North Bend, British Columbia, on October 11, 1995. In the background, CP 240617, a derelict 1929-vintage boxcar slowly reveals the "Spans the World" lettering of better days. *Greg McDonnell*

There are no secrets about the food as the waitress and cook prepare lunch—including the best minestrone west of the Great Divide—for hungry railroaders at the CP Rail North Bend Cafe at North Bend, British Columbia, on October 11, 1995. *Greg McDonnell*

Nearing Osoyoos, British Columbia, on October 20, 1964, CP H16-44 8604 trundles southward with a pair of empty eight-hatch reefers ordered for loading by Okanagan fruit-growers. *James A. Brown*

Passing lovingly tended gardens near Vedder Crossing, British Columbia, BC Hydro SW900RS's 906 and 905 work eastward with a Fraser Valley local on August 11, 1979. *Doug Phillips*

Monument at Mileage 154.5

In the predawn blackness of a January morning, BC Rail No. 28 marches out of Lillooet, British Columbia. The guttural grumbling of Alco 251's reverberates off the rock walls as M630's 710 and 715, in concert with mid-train helpers C630M 701 and M420B 685, get the southbound time freight under way. In the cab of the 710, all eyes are focused forward as headlights probe the darkness for the twisting rails of the Squamish Subdivision. Conversation in the cab suddenly stops as a chilling spectre is illuminated in the brilliant glare of the lights.

Beached on the shore of Seton Lake, the mangled carcass of wrecked BCR M630 711 lies at the water's edge like a giant piece of driftwood tossed from the lake. The cab is silent as the 710 slowly trudges past her fallen sister. Thoughts turn to the perils of mountain railroading and a February 1980 night, when the 711 and C425 808 struck a rock slide just south of here, sending both units and several cars into the cold black waters of the lake. Helped from the frigid water by the track patrolman who had inspected the line just moments before the slide, the engineer survived. The brakeman was never seen again.

Sixteen months later, salvage crews recovered the 808 from the lake. The ex-Erie Lackawanna C425 was rebuilt at Squamish and emerged from the shop as number 800. Hung up on an underwater ledge, the 711 was abandoned in its watery tomb until a pair of local divers floated the big Alco to the surface in October 1988.

For two years, the 711 sat on the shore, serving as a grim reminder of the dangers faced every day by mountain railroaders. Preserved as-is, the battered hulk would have made a fitting memorial to the dozens of mountain railroaders who have lost their lives in the line of duty, not just along Seton Lake, but throughout British Columbia. Instead, the would-be monument was cut up and hauled away for scrap in December 1990.

A monument to the mountain railroaders who have lost their lives in the line of duty, the mangled carcass of BCR M630 711 languishes on the shore of Seton Lake, just south of Lillooet, British Columbia, on January 27, 1990. The lead unit in a fatal collision with a rock slide just south of this location, the 711 was recovered after lying submerged in the lake for more than eight years. Efforts to sell the unit for salvage failed, and in December 1990, the big Alco was cut up and hauled away for scrap. *Greg McDonnell*

Viewed from the cab of wrecked BCR M630 711, southbound RDC's approach the location where the ill-fated big Alco hit a rock slide and plunged into Seton Lake in February 1980. As with all BCR trains operating over this spectacular piece of railroad, No. 2 is preceeded by a motor-car patrol to ensure the safety of the right of way. *Greg McDonnell*

A legacy of Great Northern's once-significant presence in southern B.C., Burlington Northern's Nelson Turn returns to Kettle Falls, Washington, crossing a curved wooden trestle south of Nelson, British Columbia, on July 14, 1987. The photographer climbed a tree to obtain this spectacular view of BN GP38-2 2080 and GP35 2507 working trackage that is now out of service. BN's Nelson Sub. local now turns at Salmo, British Columbia, and the railroad has filed to abandon the line beyond there. *James A. Speaker*

Nearly a continent away from its old eastern stomping grounds, ex-CP RS3 8427 works the Crown Zellerbach log dump at Ladysmith, British Columbia, on May 13, 1981. *Doug Phillips*

At the height of the short Arctic summer, wildflowers bloom as a pair of White Pass & Yukon's unique Alco-powered, shovel-nose GE's lead a freight into Carcross, Yukon, in July 1980. *Ken Goslett*

Sasha, "the Bennett dog," carefully surveys the activity at the White Pass & Yukon station in Bennett, British Columbia, on October 11, 1981. "Whose dog is it?" the photographer asked. To which a veteran railroader replied: "She's the Bennett dog. As long as I've been here, there's always been a Bennett dog." *David R. Busse*

Under Sasha's watchful eye, White Pass & Yukon GE's 100, 94, 99 and 95 bring a train of ore cars into Bennett, British Columbia, on October 11, 1981. *David R. Busse*

Special thanks to the railroaders, photographers and friends
who generously contributed to this volume.

Steve Bradley
Alvin H. Brown
James A. Brown
Dave Busse
Tom Carver
H. R. Clarke
John Denison
Robert J. Gallagher
John F. Garden
Steve Glischinski
Ken Goslett
Doug Harrop

Philip R. Hastings
Matthew J. Herson, Jr.
Brian Jennision
Brad Jolliffe
J. Parker Lamb
Robert Lambrecht
Tom Lambrecht
Bill Linley
John C. Lucas
Robert R. Malinoski
Philip Mason
Jeff Mast

Amber McCorkindale
Andrew McDonnell
George McDonnell
Maureen McDonnell
Joe McMillan
George F. Melvin
Paul Meyer
William D. Miller
Mark Perry
Doug Phillips
Hal Reiser
Newton Rossiter

Robert Sandusky
Jim Shaughnessy
Dave Shaw
Stan J. Smaill
James A. Speaker
Dave Stanley
Andrew Sutherland
John Sutherland
James Van Brocklin
John Barras Walker
Richard Yaremko